Bittersweet
A Daughter's Memoir

Marilyn Arnold

All Rights Reserved and Assigned to:
Mayhaven Publishing, Inc.
PO Box 557
Mahomet, IL 61853

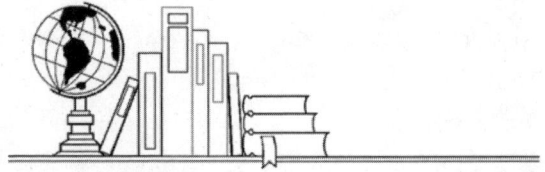

Cover Design: Doris Wenzel
Copyright © 2010 Marilyn Arnold
First Edition - First Printing 2010
ISBN 10: 1-932278-52-4
ISBN 13: 978-1-932278-52-1
Library of Congress Control Number: 2010927264

Note: On the cover and title page, a photo of Rhoda Clark before she became Rhoda Clark Arnold—in her twenties.

Photo and story on page 188 reprinted with permission, courtesy of Brigham Young University *Daily Universe*.

Prologue

Actually, Mother, this Prologue is an afterthought, but what I say here needs to be said up front because times have changed quite drastically since the writing of some parts of this memoir. The dreaded and foreseeable Recession, with a capital "R," hit the world and changed the mind-set and habits of a good many people. The rampant consumerism, the high living (often on credit) that seemed to define our society and make it so different from the world that you and I shared when I was a child, has been tamed by hard times. The future has become uncertain and full of fear. Consequently, some of my then quite legitimate comparisons between "the present" and an earlier day may now seem a bit naive. Many of the comparisons, however, are implicit rather than explicit because they merely describe a simpler, far less affluent time without reference to the twenty-first century.

I was tempted to go back and revise some of my observations to reflect the huge turn in the country's fortunes

Marilyn Arnold

beginning in 2008 or thereabouts, but then I thought better of it. As the text stands, a piece of it reflects a recent reality of our day that we shouldn't forget. The narrative offers occasional snapshots of a flush time that I suppose many of us thought would go on forever. It is a reminder of how irresponsible a lot of us have been, and how fast we can tumble when we throw prudence to the wind. And when we put our trust in people who promise us wildly exaggerated returns for our investments, or who encourage us to buy luxuries and homes far beyond our means. Yes, Mother, we should have known better. And if you had lived to see the loss of reason and control, you would have sounded the warning. You had seen too much of lean times. You would have known the bubble had to burst. "Frugality" was ever your watchword, and you would have weathered the storm better than most.

The trouble, of course, is that many people are being hurt who are not at fault. A whole society suffers when financial foundations crumble. May all of us, through my personal journey into memory, remember that hard times have come before. May we remember that lean times were long a way of life for many of us, and for our parents and our parents' parents. May we remember that the truly good times were times when our role models were heroes in the finest sense—models of goodness, models of courage, models of humility. They were not shallow, self-centered celebrities; raunchy, foul-mouthed rock stars; or pampered, overpaid athletes.

Bittersweet

Well, enough said, Mother. Maybe too much. And so on with our story, yours and mine. On with the pages torn from the book of our lives.

Left to right: The Arnold family, Rey, Rhoda (Mother), Marilyn, H. Lynn (Dad), and Ned at our home in Ogden, Utah.

Marilyn Arnold

A family portrait: Rey in front, flanked by Marilyn and Mother (Rhoda). Ned and Dad (H. Lynn Arnold) are standing.

Page One

I remember it as though it were yesterday. I was in ninth grade, junior high at that time in my school district. A classmate and sometime friend, a girl in the "cool" crowd (I'll call her Susan), had come over to my house one Saturday afternoon. As a rule, I managed to connect with her and her clique of friends only peripherally. This was partly because our family couldn't afford the Jantzen sweaters and White Stag clothing required for solid membership in that group, and partly because I was a designated "goody-goody" girl—meaning I didn't swear and wouldn't touch alcohol or tobacco. (Drugs had not yet made the scene in Ogden City Schools.)

Furthermore, I wasn't allowed to attend unsupervised parties. Period. Boys who were drawn to those kinds of things, and the experimental beer and promiscuity that went with them, weren't interested in me. Which was just as well because I was not permitted to be interested in them. You, Mother, were very strict, and so was Dad. The kids who ran with the "in" crowd seemed to have a lot more freedom and a lot more fun than I did, and I envied them. I didn't know at the time how fortunate I was. I got a fleeting sense of it that particular Saturday, however.

While Susan and I sat on a little slope of grass that reached from the front of our modest brick and stucco house to the sidewalk, you and Dad backed down the narrow driveway that ran alongside the slope. That is, Dad was backing our black 1936 Plymouth, which was ancient by any standards, and you were in the passenger seat. (Our next car was a white 1949 Ford.) You didn't drive, though once upon a time you had a driver's license. Dad stopped adjacent to us and asked if there was anything in particular I wanted from the grocery store. Then you leaned across him and spoke to Susan.

"How about you, Susan? What may we bring you from the store?" Any normal mother would have said, "what *can* we bring," but not you. You, Mother, were precise about such things, fussy beyond reason, I thought. When I would ask, "Can I" do such and such, something I needed permission for—which was virtually everything!—you would invariably respond, "You *can*, but you *may* not." Meaning I was physically and mentally able to do whatever it was, but did not have permission, at least not until I asked with correct grammatical usage.

As we watched you and Dad drive down the street on your weekly errand, Susan said quietly, "You're so lucky to

Bittersweet

have parents like yours." Susan had no siblings and no idea where her father was. Her relationship with her mother and recent stepfather was difficult at best. She herself, who was bright and academically promising, quit school after tenth grade to marry an older fellow. He ran with a rather wild crowd, and those were the fellows she hung out with, beginning in seventh or eighth grade. Her life with him, I later learned, was nothing but heartache. I have long since lost track of her, but I have never forgotten what she said that long ago day.

How different my life might have been with another kind of mother, with one who didn't keep a tight rein on a high-spirited daughter. You never gave me the freedom I thought I wanted, the freedom with which I would probably have ruined my life.

Incidentally, Mother, you must have been aware that only one or two of the girls in that junior high school "in" crowd I so much envied went on to high school, let alone college. The rest married older boys, and nearly all of them wound up with babies and errant husbands in their mid-to late-teens.

Maybe the indefinable hold you had on me, on my mind and heart, kept me in line when as a teenager yearning for popularity (that shallow, transitory illusion that keeps celebrities in adolescence) I might have grown careless. All my life, Mother, even in my self-absorbed teen years, I could handle almost anything except your tears. I rarely saw you cry, but when I did, it tore me apart. Still vivid in memory is one night in particular when my immature thoughtlessness wracked you with worry. I had never seen you cry like that before, except over your soldier son, and I have never seen you cry like that since. I was fifteen or sixteen and had gone out with a boyfriend to some event or gathering. When my curfew hour arrived, I had not arrived home—I who had always been dependable in such matters. Nearly two hours passed, and I was still not home. When my beau of the moment walked me to the door, we were met by Dad. The boy culprit beat a hasty retreat, leaving me to face the music alone.

There was no anger expressed. You were in tears, so broken by worry that you could scarcely speak. And I could tell that you had been crying for a long time. You could only imagine that something terrible had happened to me. Dad said he called the police to ask about reported accidents, and he hugged me in immense, solemn relief. But he was not happy with me, oh no. I remember vowing that night never to do that to you again, Mother, and I never did. I was never late again, not even ten minutes, that I didn't call you and tell you that I was running late, and that was before cell phones. (Incidentally, my younger brother reminds me that it was the

Bittersweet

same for him. He avows that not wanting to hurt you was the principal corrective force in his life, the thing that kept him on the "straight and narrow.")

Your face of that night haunts me still. It is one of those things for which I have never forgiven myself. Maybe that was the night I discovered how much I loved you, and how much you loved me. I went to bed full of remorse. I think I grew up a little that night. Whatever it was, luck or Providence, you were my mother, and that (as Robert Frost would have said) has made all the difference. I have often wished I could go back and do it all over. Get it right this time, my life with you, Mother. Show my love openly and often, from my junior high school years until your death at age ninety-one. Do most women wish for such? Did you with grandmother? Did you with me?

Once I graduated from childhood, we were always a little formal, Mother, you and I. We were almost close, but not quite. Rarely at serious odds, but reserved. I never heard you raise your voice, not once, not to anyone. I raised mine to you once, just once, when I was thirteen or fourteen, and I have never forgotten it. I still feel the shame, though what I said was mild by today's standards. You were on my case about something, an uncompleted chore perhaps; and I, not thinking, carelessly replied, "Oh, don't get your ear twisted"—an expression I had heard somewhere and now had an opportunity to use. It was a mistake. You, Mother, simply stopped what you were doing, looked at me in disappointed disbelief, and said very quietly, "Marilyn, I'm surprised." That was all, and that was enough. I was crushed to the core. What happened after that is a blur, as undoubtedly were my eyes. I don't even remember if I apologized. All I remember is what I said and what you said and how terrible I felt.

The love between us was immense, Mother, but almost never verbally expressed. Now I want to express it, over and over, a hundred times a day, and it is too late. The loyalty was matchless, but not told in words. It's as if we had taken a vow of silence on the matter of our affection and the inner lives we didn't, or couldn't, share.

Now I ask myself why. Now I have this need to tell you of my real life and to learn of yours, and it is too late. We lived and spoke across an invisible barrier, embarrassed at feelings, reluctant to uncover our own real selves, much less the real self of the other.

Of course, we knew the love was there, silently sustaining us. We never questioned the love. You might say we took it for granted and knew we could rely on it. It was that strong. But why did I never hold you close and tell you I loved you? Why only the quick, safe hugs? Why did I not comprehend your sorrows? Why did I run from them, not wanting to lift the lids of their frightening boxes? And why

Bittersweet

did you not comprehend mine? (Or did you, but kept silent?) In all our talk, why did we not talk of things that really mattered? Of things harbored in our deepest souls? I think we were afraid. Not so much of each other as of our own selves. Of looking at our feelings in the open. What might we discover and disclose if we opened that door? What might we learn and not be able to forget?

I came closest to finding you the day you died. I arrived at your bedside unable to believe you were letting go, that this was indeed the moment of dread. (You had long since retired and moved to a duplex in Orem, but now you were in a care center.) I had been with you short hours before, talking our usual talk—of Dad's being off on a little outing in the care center van, of your frustrating and exhausting night in a chair where careless licensed care givers had forgotten you, of your medications and which ones were running low, of your concerns about the home you had left just six weeks before. We both knew that you and Dad would never return to live there again, but we didn't speak those words. We couldn't. To speak them would have been to confirm a terrible truth. The truth that your life as you had known it and cherished it was essentially over. The truth that what we were to do now was to endure and wait. I could not face that truth any more than you could. So we played the game of evasion. We were good at it. Well practiced. But now, the game was over.

You were unconscious, lying there so still, so peaceful, really. The oxygen concentrator was huffing its customary rhythm, filling the room with its bleak necessity. I lay beside you, something I hadn't done since I was a small child. Why hadn't we sprawled on the grass on starry summer nights and talked about nothing and everything? Why hadn't we sat over soggy morning cereal and opened the pages of living stories? Why hadn't we taken long walks together in the foothills, or the canyon, and rejoiced at the sight of a red-shafted flicker, or a brilliant western tanager?

Why hadn't I held you while you wept over your first-born son's departure in an Army uniform, and over the death of your mother? Why didn't I fully grasp the suffering produced by your disabled heart, and then your disabling stroke? Why was I embarrassed by your seldom seen tears? Why did I back off, bewildered, unable to give comfort? Why didn't I fully appreciate what macular degeneration and lost vision cost you, and how Dad's lost mind drained energy from you every hour? Now, too late, I marvel at your courage, your incredible strength, your desire to protect me from your sorrows.

Then, too, why hadn't I told you that my marriage was a terrible mistake, a disaster, and asked you to comfort me? Was it because we didn't know how to share tears, or because I assumed that in your disappointment (and your concern for family and neighborhood opinion) you couldn't understand? Was it because all my life I had felt the weight (a better word than "burden") of your expectations? Was it because the driving force behind all I ever achieved was the desire to please you? You were not a large, imposing woman. Why was I always afraid of incurring your displeasure?

There was no meanness in you, so I had no fear of physical punishment or deprivation. There was only a quiet strength and rectitude the likes of which I have rarely encountered again in a whole lifetime. Dad was strong, too, but he could be explosive. You, by contrast, were the power of an explosion that never happened and never would, held in abeyance but known to be there. No, that's not quite right either. You, in fact, were the power of tranquility, the power of self control, which is stronger by far than any overt demonstration of force. And, as your lastborn son puts it, you were entirely without guile.

Lying beside you in that institution of lost hope, taking your smooth, almost transparent hand in mine, Mother, I was so full of tenderness and fear that I thought my heart would break. We came together at that moment, you and I, and I became your child once more. No longer adult daughter, so good at elusion (pretending normalcy), empty assurances, busyness, grocery lists, errands, phone calls, and transportation to the doctor and pharmacy. Those things were done, finished, and the time had come to recapture the child-mother and the child-daughter in us.

I was aware of your meager breathing, of the anguish released with it from your face, of the tension gone from your body, of your incredible frailty and agonizing dearness. We lay there together a long time, almost breathing as one. I don't know if you felt it, though somewhere inside me I sensed that you did. I wept in silent recognition of the holiness of that moment, a moment outside time. Why, Mother, did you have to leave me in order for me to find you?

And then your breathing ceased, left my breathing, and I felt your hand grow cool in my unbelieving fingers. It was over. You crossed into eternity with the ease of a graceful figure skater shifting effortlessly into reverse. You seemed to know the way, and I lay there, an astonished witness to the miracle.

Other memories associated with your passing keep rising to the surface of my mind, Mother. I was living nearly 300 miles away when your troubles began. I had moved to the desert when all was well and your personal needs were less pressing than when Dad was undergoing cancer treatment. It was your firstborn son who stepped up to the plate in my absences. He came to your rescue countless times, and cared for you in ways that probably surprised both you and him. (An unacknowledged distance had grown between the two of you over the years.) I traveled to you often and stayed long, especially in that last difficult year. But it was he who became your mainstay in your great need, who allowed himself to become again your dear, dear son. It was he who could now show his love openly and accept your love openly.

Still vivid is the anguish of the decision to search out a care center where you and Dad would be safe from the perils of unfriendly stairways and the worries associated with home ownership and maintenance. Where the touch of a button could bring help within minutes. Dad, who became a "frequent flyer" (that is, *faller*) at home, had long since lost the ability to manage anything more demanding than getting himself into shirt and pants every morning and into pajamas every night. (Now I think of it, it seemed a bit odd to me that Dad always slept with his pajama tops tucked in, the same way he wore his shirts. I don't believe I ever saw Dad with a shirttail out. He never submitted to jeans or T-shirts, either, nor did he ever wear anything but leather shoes on his feet. No sneakers for him, much less sandals. Even his house slippers were leather, though in later years he rarely bothered with them. He went from shoes to bed with no lounging about the house in between.)

Marilyn Arnold

We settled on "assisted living," which allowed you the freedom and privacy of a small apartment and, at the same time, the security of trained aides 24/7. Theoretically, at least. Your firstborn son had three husky boys, and all of them were on hand to haul furniture and boxes. Twice, as it turned out, and then again when the end came and the house had to be emptied. Only one son of your lastborn child lived in the West and he helped when he could break away from his medical training.

The first ten days went reasonably well. You, Mother, had couch, chairs, table, and bed from home. Your own things. Dad seemed a little confused at first, but settled into his favorite chair in front of the window and seemed to conclude that he was still in the house off 800 North, and that his old Ford Ltd. was in the garage just beyond the wall. His security blanket, that Ford. He hadn't driven it for nearly ten years, but he would never consent to its sale. He insisted that he still drove it daily, for short errands around town, to the bank and the doctor and the grocery store.

But then you, Mother, went into congestive heart failure, and we nearly lost you. We didn't dare leave you alone after that episode, even for a moment. The wife of your firstborn, she who is a most faithful and able watcher and tender, alternated night duty with me while your son relieved us during the day. Finally, we arranged to move you and Dad out of assisted living and into a room where you could receive

Bittersweet

more constant care. And you did receive loving care from several dear women. It was just that one night, the night before your death, someone left you in a chair and forgot about you. Left you without your oxygen and without access to a call button. You sat there all night, unable to sleep, unable to summon help, unable to rise on your own. I think that is the night you threw in the towel, gave up the fight. It may have been an unconscious decision, but it was a decision nonetheless.

You always said that you wanted to live just one day longer than Dad. You wanted to see him through. You knew he was helpless without you. But you reached the end of your will that night, Mother. The next day you made your exit. You finally found the door. As for your desire to stay the course with Dad, you nearly made it. He died just one month and one day after you left us. Again, your firstborn son and I found ourselves making arrangements for that second event. I remember hearing him remark, "I hadn't expected to be on a first name basis with my mortician." Your lastborn son was as true and fine as his brother, but he lived on the eastern end of the continent. He came, of course, both times, as did his wife and family.

One thing about those traumatic days, days when fluids filled your lungs and swelled your limbs, stays with me, haunts me. One thing, especially. Helpless and frighteningly near death, you allowed me to feed you, one spoonful at a time. You lay there on your familiar sofa in unfamiliar surroundings, wholly needful. And I, I was so full of fear that I could scarcely steady the spoon. But with each bite, as you swallowed with effort, you said, "Thank you." Even under those circumstances, you expressed gratitude. You, Mother, were incapable of ingratitude. If I take no other lesson from you, may I take that lesson.

When the day of your death (May 28, 1998) finally came to a close, Mother, I went wearily, sorrowfully, incredulously, to your home, to the basement bedroom where I took up quarters when I was in town. Still scarcely able to believe, much less comprehend, what had happened, I numbly prepared for bed. The street light cast an eerie glow through the small window, making faintly visible the items your hands had placed on the inexpensive but serviceable blonde dresser that once sat in my little Ogden bedroom. These items were things you no longer wished to display upstairs, but out of fondness and long association could not discard. I lay through the long night, unable to close my eyes, much less sleep, staring alternately at the ceiling, the window, the chest of drawers, and the dresser.

Several times I left the bed and went to the dresser, where I picked up items touched by your hands. Treasures all. Funny, for several years after that night I saw those things

Bittersweet

clearly in my mind, and their placement on the dresser, but now only three images remain: an ivory-colored doily you crocheted once upon a time, a small sky-blue ceramic dish with a delicately sculpted pink rose on its lid, and a white ceramic bud vase with gold (paint) trim and pink roses and trailing leaves sculpted on the front. Roses. Your signature flower, Mother.

Even as I lay in bed or touched your ceramic roses, the living roses you cared for so faithfully and tenderly were blooming hugely, beautifully along the driveway outside. I probably planted them (being fairly adept with a shovel) since I lived in the north half of the duplex we shared for several years before I moved on. Yes, I pruned them, too, but they were your roses. You even talked to them to encourage their growth and prosperity. (You also talked to the little aspen trees transplanted from a friend's mountain property. They got the message and thrived almost too well!) I remember the name of only one rose, the Peace Rose. You knew them all by name and lineage.

As the years pass, Mother, you are with me not less, but more. Someone said that a woman knows she is past fifty when she puts her arm in her sleeve and her mother's hand comes out. However old she is, a woman lives forever with her mother, in a sense becomes her mother. I have found that

Marilyn Arnold

although the years fly by and the pages turn, the remembering goes on, becoming more insistent as undefined spectres of my own inevitable end begin their phantom dance on the ever approaching horizon. Shadows of the past and future converge. Your life, that never fully merged with mine when it might have counted, is today occupying space that I wish I had given it years ago. Why, Mother, didn't I let myself know you, and let you know me? We didn't quarrel. We didn't criticize. Maybe I'd have known you better if we had.

What might you have taught me if all those years I had listened with more than ears of flesh? Why is it that only in late adulthood (I'm not saying how late) I remember the really important things about you? Why did I not consciously recognize that you never, ever stooped to gossip, or uttered a coarse or profane word? And that lying was as foreign to you as Arabic? Did I assume that these traits of character merely constituted standard "mother" behavior? And now, as you haunt my reveries, I long to start over with you, to scroll back to the time when we knew each other with few complications, when the idea of human perfection and mortal achievement scarcely crossed our minds, much less our conversations. When there was no such thing between us as pride, much less prejudice. The time, of course, was my childhood.

Bittersweet

The family at Mother's funeral.

Marilyn Arnold

Marilyn, Ned, Dad (H. Lynn), and Rey after Mother's funeral. We would be attending Dad's funeral just one month later.

Page Two

Go back with me now, Mother, to that little house I spoke of earlier, a house squeezed among others on a tar and chipped-rock street in the working class neighborhood where you and Dad lived for thirty-four years. The three of us, my two brothers and I, scarcely remember any other home. (It never occurred to us that a home might have more than one bathroom. We were glad enough that, unlike Grandmother's rustic facility, it was indoors and had running water.) That is where the shaping events of my life occurred. That is where you and I shared something precious, before we began playing a role for each other, the role we thought was expected of us. The role we thought would protect us from hurting either ourselves or each other. That time predates the days of formalities. Why do some mothers and daughters enter an era of formalities? Why do the teen years change everything forever? But, I'm getting ahead of myself.

Marilyn Arnold

Even now, I see the house clearly, just as it was (and still is, pretty much, to my surprise and joy—an old neighbor sent me a recent picture just last year). Rough, deep red brick began above the gray painted concrete foundation and met what must have been stucco on the upper half. Not today's nubby fashionable stucco, but a composition made somewhat smooth, either by intention or as a result of repeated coats of cream-colored paint (now given over to white by the current occupants). It had a front porch, as nearly all homes of that era and social class did, a porch partially enclosed by a waist-high (your waist, Mother, not mine) brick wall and two square brick columns.

Inside the column at the top of the porch stairs hung an old black mailbox on a rusty nail. The postman (it was always a post*man* in those days) had to climb the stairs to leave the mail (penny postcards from Grandmother and envelopes bearing three-cent stamps), at our house and at nearly every other house on the street. Only now do I wonder how he felt about that, if he got tired of daily climbing all those stairs with his mailbag on his shoulder. In those days, the postman walked his route, stopping at every residence, knowing intimately every yard and every nasty-tempered dog.

In my childhood, Mother, a front porch was a special place. People of our station (I nearly said "ilk," but thought

Bittersweet

better of it) didn't have backyard patios, they had front porches. We gave no thought to outdoor barbecuing or walled off family space. Children could roam from backyard to backyard with few barriers to impede them, and rear alleyways were often handier than sidewalks. A patio party was for rich people in movies, not for people like us; and privacy sounded downright snooty. What we wanted was the feeling of community. We belonged not just to ourselves, but to everyone on the street, except a couple of grumps.

Front porches were for sitting on and calling to neighbors from, friends who were out for a stroll in the cool of a summer evening. Central air conditioning, like television, would eventually overtake us, but not in the house of my childhood. Is central air to blame for the loss of front porches, and for the demise of easy conversation as the day cooled and the sun sank behind the small frame house across the street? Is it to blame for the fact that we no longer know all our neighbors, or that children no longer play "Mother, May I?" on front porch steps, or "Kick the Can" or "Hide-n-Seek" as the rosy dusk settles on summer streets?

Today, with air conditioning, people close their doors and windows in summer as well as winter. You kept ours open, Mother, to catch a breeze. I don't remember suffering from the heat. What I do remember is your calling to Mrs. Stone across our slender driveway, open window to open window. And I remember summer afternoons spent lying under the

Marilyn Arnold

round, bushy tree that pretty much filled the Stones's front lawn, listening to their daughter, Anna, some years older than I, play the piano. Their front door was open, naturally, and I thought Anna played beautifully. The only song I remember from her repertoire was "The Missouri Waltz." I used to lie there, undiscovered, silently begging her to play the tune again and again. And then one day it arrived, our own piano. Not new, naturally, but Grandmother's, from your childhood home—a small farmhouse with coal stove for cooking and heating, no plumbing, and multitudes of children. I could take piano lessons now, traveling alone by bus and transfer ticket to a teacher many miles away. I could learn to play "The Missouri Waltz."

It was a little joke between you and me that you could play one piece on the piano. I can still see you, sitting there at Grandmother's big upright in what had been our dining room, smiling as you plinked out your one tune, "Catch the Sunshine," on page fourteen of the old *Deseret Sunday School Song Book*. That song had no sharps or flats and no fancy stuff. Simple and melodic it was, like you, Mother. (I just checked to make certain that I had the page right—I did—and saw that in that old tan song book of yours, page fourteen is torn and smudged and dog-eared, and has, in fact, been taped together in several places. You must have played that song many times, or maybe I took it up early on, too. Anyway, we nearly wore that page to shreds! I see these words inscribed on the inside

Bittersweet

cover: "Aug. 21, 1931. Presented to Sister Rhoda Clark Arnold by the Lehi Fourth Ward Sunday School Officers and Teachers for her Faithful Service.")

You see, Mother, in those days, I led a charmed life. Oh, there were the occasional spats with my brothers, but you never allowed those spats to get out of hand. You smoothed the waters of my childhood with your gentle ways and soft voice. Gentleness notwithstanding, I always knew you were in charge. There was never any doubt of that. You meant business. You knew the wisdom of the saying in Proverbs 15:1: "A soft answer turneth away wrath."

Today, I see you in myself, Mother. Not only in the hand emerging from my sleeve, but in countless other ways. We were so different, you and I, and yet not so different after all. Like you, I am highstrung, a worrier, and yes, a fussbudget. How can that be, given that I have always been outdoorsy and athletic and seemingly unflappable? Well, it turns out that I am very flappable, but I conceal it better than you did. In fact, in high school and college, I fancied myself a jokester and a party animal, pulling pranks that you would not have approved of. (Did you ever play tricks or steal watermelons, Mother? Were you foolishly young once?) A few of us—girls, all—had a lovely time one summer making mischief at the expense of our junior college friends. The harmless, inconvenient sort of mischief. I lived at home with you and Dad and my younger brother through junior college, but I never told you about those pranks, did I?

Here I must insert a digression (the first of many, I fear). I distinctly remember an outdoor party in one of the canyons above Ogden. While the boys and other girls (we didn't think of ourselves as "men" and "women" back then) were roasting hotdogs and singing to the strums of ukuleles, a few of us (with one turncoat male) sneaked away and removed a hubcap or two from all the cars, including cars belonging to the boys we came with. (To avoid suspicion, you see.) These chrome disks we mixed up and put in a pile in the middle of the parking area before sneaking back to the group.

Two fellows had been posted below to watch roads, to be on the lookout for rival fraternity boys who might be expected to appear and pull tricks. Our guys were not prepared for an inside job, however, and we got away with it. Why couldn't I go home and share riotous laughter with you over such an escapade, Mother? I was certain then that you would not have enjoyed the joke, that you would have been chagrined. Now I wonder if I underestimated you, in that and other things.

In spite of our worry-wart similarities, I still sometimes ask myself how a daughter like me could have issued from

Bittersweet

a mother like you. Our differences were huge. We never even looked alike. I grew tall and lean, tanned, built for basketball, tennis, hiking, skiing, and reaching things on high shelves. You were never tall, even before your frame collapsed with osteoporosis. You were proper, fussy, and quiet-mannered; I am casual, distinctly unfrilled, and rather noisy. I never saw you in jeans or sweats or shorts or T-shirts, my attire of choice even now. But this does not mean you were a stranger to college athletics. Hardly.

Your sports interests, however, were rather narrowly defined and were of the spectator variety. For years they consisted solely of almost unparalleled enthusiasm for Brigham Young University basketball (with a little to spare for the Ogden Reds baseball team). Why, my brothers and I were reared on BYU basketball via KSL radio (in those days, there was no such thing as intercollegiate women's basketball). I still remember the names of at least two players from my childhood—Mel Hutchins and Roland Minson. Some years later, when BYU began fielding respectable football teams, you expanded your sports allegiance to include them. I think Steve Young won you over.

Not being a hiker, and having zero tolerance for dirt, and no desire whatsoever to sleep on the ground in any bag, let alone an unlaundered one, you never understood my passion for backpacking. And we never went camping as a family. You always said that you had finally, in adulthood, acquired running water, central heat, a bathroom, and a kitchen with a gas range and a refrigerator. You did not intend to camp unless you could take all those conveniences along.

You played no sports, but in retirement you moved to Utah County where you cultivated a productive garden and regularly walked the extended neighborhood at an impressive clip. You always said proudly that when you walked you walked fast, you didn't "mess around." (I'm quoting you, Mother. You did say "mess around.") After your vision all but left you, Mother, you still walked your two miles daily. Even a bad spill or two, over a child's toy left on a sidewalk, didn't slow you down for long. I was never sure that Dad shared your enthusiasm for the walking routine, but he went along with it. He liked your company.

And yes, Mother, you were domestic. I confess that I am not. I dutifully attended junior high school sewing and cooking classes, but they didn't, as we say when speaking of vaccinations and other such unpleasantries, "take." And the older I get, the less inclined I am to cook anything but soup, and that only in cold weather. The microwave oven is my appliance of choice for meal preparation; and fruits, salads, and whole grain breads (and chocolate) are the principal accompaniments to my soup. That said, however, your habitual thrift in domestic matters (and all other matters, even when no longer driven by necessity) has somehow lodged itself in many of my practices. Except early on in the buying of clothes. There was a time in my professional life (from which aberration I have since recovered) when I bought many fine clothes. The result of that period of temporary insanity is that I still own many fine clothes. The same ones. These days I hate to shop, I passionately hate to shop, so I rarely do it.

I think that you, Mother, liked to shop. What you didn't like was to spend. That reluctance was still ingrained when money became less tight in your later years. I've never known you to spend a dollar on yourself without entering into serious and extended self-debate. Sometimes days of self-debate. For Dad and me, shopping with you was pure misery, elongated, maddening misery. We were much relieved when you moved to the town where your youngest sister lived. She, who understood your shopping practices completely because she too was afflicted with indecision in such matters, happily inherited that assignment. I still marvel that, on occasion, you actually bought clothes that you did not return the next day. I can't recall a time when you weren't fully clothed.

You accepted the fact that your only daughter never bought yard goods, not despite but possibly *because* I wore home-made clothes and hand-me-downs from a neighbor all my young life. Even today, sewing on a button raises my blood pressure a few notches. I can still see you, Mother, sitting at the kitchen table before your old White portable sewing machine, making shirts for the boys and dresses, tops, and bibbed pants (we called them "jammies") for me. Then there was that beautiful red velvet coat and matching bonnet trimmed with white fur (fake, of course), made for my two-year-old-body. Oh, how I hated to grow out of that beautiful coat. You splurged on that coat, Mother. I know it now if I didn't then. Naturally, you also made pajamas (didn't we call them "jammies" too?) for all of us except Dad. I never asked why he got store-bought pajamas and barber shop haircuts when the rest of us didn't. It seems heads of household were entitled to certain privileges. (I can still see my brothers on a stool in the kitchen as you worked around their heads, squeezing the handles of the old manual clippers.)

In fact, in one dresser drawer in my guest bedroom at this very moment are three pairs of knee-length summer pajamas that you made for me when I was full-grown and employed and well able to purchase such items. I wore them until your vision left, but after that, when I knew there would be no more pajamas, I put them away. Now they will never wear out. I will always have them, aqua-, pink-, and tan-checked. They are a connection between us, for they were made out of love rather than frugality. As I think about it now, Mother, maybe love was always behind your sewing, love in addition to economy. In such acts, in doing rather than in talking, you always expressed your affection. And maybe I followed your example. Then why do I so long for the talking now, and why do my eyes fill when I open a drawer and see those pajamas, made for me when your eyes could see? Why does my hand tremble when I touch them?

I also remember when money was so scarce that you did not even buy a thirty-five-cent pattern for a boy's shirt or a girl's dress unless it was absolutely necessary. You borrowed patterns from Mrs. Schneiter across the street. She was an accomplished seamstress and had many patterns on hand, for girls and for growing boys like yours. You would then cut your own newspaper patterns from hers, first drawing their outlines on the paper. How well I remember seeing you on hands and knees on the linoleum floor of our spare kitchen, measuring tape at hand, placing home-cut newspaper patterns this way and that, working to find the layout that would require the least amount of cloth. Then you would measure carefully, never buying an inch more material than was needed.

I remember, too, in second or third grade, we were to make button boxes at school for our mothers as a Christmas surprise. The boxes were to be fashioned from a small Planter's peanut can (metal, in those days), which each student had to provide. On visits to the grocery store, we children had seen indulgences like canned peanuts on the shelves but had never dared ask for such, just to eat ourselves and not to save for company. But I had to have the can, for purposes I was instructed not to divulge. You and Dad consented, and we brought the tin treasure home, to relish every roasted nut and to feel like royalty.

Marilyn Arnold

With pride, I carried my empty washed can to school and painted it bright red. I then pasted little stickers on it and wrapped it. How pleased you seemed to get it, and you promptly transferred your saved buttons from their old box into that can. Any item of clothing that had grown too small or could bear no further mending or patching was given to Grandmother for quilt blocks, but not before the buttons were removed and saved for future use. Nothing was wasted in our house, nothing. Not even time.

And especially not electricity or food or heat. I grew up turning lights out, closing off rooms not used during the day, quickly closing outside doors in winter, saving string on a pencil spindle, squeezing tooth paste from the bottom of the tube and rolling the tube, cleaning my plate at supper. There you have it—the *you* in me. I still turn out lights, close doors, and roll the toothpaste tube from the bottom.

But some of those thrifty practices have their tender side. I remember cold winter nights, Mother, when I crawled beneath shivery sheets in my unheated bedroom, eager to see you come through the door with stove-heated towels to wrap around my feet. How snug you made me feel! And how loved. The three of us children shared that tiny room until it was decided that your growing daughter needed a little privacy. A small room was carved out in the basement, and it became "the boys room," off limits to sisters and other under-aged females. It wasn't heated either, and I never knew if you

Bittersweet

extended the hot towel service to the basement.

Where, I wonder, is the line between wisely "frugal" and downright "cheap"? Even now, Mother, I sit here in February in "sweat pants," long-sleeved T-shirt under heavy flannel shirt, wool socks, and fur-lined slippers. My typical winter uniform when at home. Now, I could boost the thermostat a couple of degrees and be more comfortable, but your genes in me dictate saving fuel and therefore money that today I could well afford to spend. Still, I can't do it. And the same thing happens in the summer, only in reverse. I acclimate myself to warmer indoor temperatures to save electricity. As it turns out, these practices suit my "green" conservationist bent, but I did such things long before we worried much about carbon footprints and limited fuel supplies. I have always done them. (Incidentally, Mother, would you consider it an act of insurrection if I confess that I just now stood and raised the thermostat one degree? Why not two? I don't know. One is all that in good conscience I can allow myself.)

Household economies aside, it shouldn't surprise you that I stretch a lot of years and miles out of an automobile. (After all, I *am* your daughter.) And I rarely buy a brand new auto. Late-model-used is my usual compromise. I am the proud owner of a 1989 red Toyota pickup. Four-cylinder, four-wheel-drive. That truck and I began our life together when it registered just over five thousand miles on its odometer. I intend to keep it until I die, at the very least. And then, I'd like to be buried in it, if that can be arranged. That vehicle is my ticket to the back country, for the best hiking and skiing anyone ever dreamed of. I have a bicycle, too, not new by any means, but serviceable. You were not happy when I bought that truck, Mother, but you became accustomed to it. It was all right for other women to drive trucks, but not *your* daughter.

It just occurs to me that the only bicycle I rode while living under your roof, Mother, was not a late-model-used, but a very *early*-model-used two-wheeler. It was a repainted hand-me-down from the "Missouri Waltz" neighbor next door. It preceded the era of three- and-ten- and fifteen-speeds, and consequently never needed tune-ups or adjustments or repairs. Unless I picked up a nail or puncture weed somewhere. I can see it yet, dull home-painted black frame with chrome fenders and scratched handlebars. No showcase model by the time I inherited it, but it worked, and I pedaled everywhere. I believe it had new handgrips, but I could be wrong about that. I was nine years old—the magic age in our family for bicycle eligibility. The old clamp-on roller skates were relegated to outer darkness beneath the basement stairs. I had arrived. Now that I think of it, Mother, I never saw you ride a bicycle, much less climb aboard a pair of roller skates.

Bittersweet

When it comes to thrift, I confess that despite your training and example, I have my weak spots. You had none, Mother, at least none that showed. But then, you never had the opportunity to be tempted by a trip through Costco or Trader Joe's. Would you have held firm and picked up only the Bolt Farms Carrot Juice or the Trader Joe's Soybean Butter that was the original purpose of your errand? I like to think you would have weakened as I invariably do, filling your basket with other delicacies, but in my heart of hearts I really don't believe it. For starters, you would never buy carrots in liquid form. I readily confess that I have not your strength and your resolve. But I want you to know that I feel a twinge of daughterly guilt when I push my cart out of Costco or Trader Joe's. I may abandon resolve in those stores, but conscience remains, part of my legacy from you. Luckily for my pocketbook, the nearest Trader Joe's is in Las Vegas.

You might be surprised to know (or would you?) that expensive tech toys appeal to me not at all. I am right-brained to a fault. Do I get that from you? Or are you disappointed that the computer and I meet only for word-processing, and that iPods and wiis and all the rest of it are a mystery? Shoot, I even cancelled all but basic cable awhile back because I don't watch the tube enough to justify the extra twenty-five bucks a month. Now, I ask you, would twenty-five dollars break me? I certainly hope not. It's the principle of the thing. Or is it? Maybe it's just the skinflint in me. Two dollars a day for television that I rarely watch. No, it's not that entirely either. What I can't stand, Mother, is waste. That is the *You* in me.

Perhaps the ultimate in economizing in my young life was forced upon us by war. Nowadays, Mother, we fight wars willy-nilly, whenever a president gets an itch to remake the world in his own image. In modern warfare we Americans take fathers and mothers from their families and sacrifice lives, but the well-heeled among us (and even the average-heeled) preserve our rich diets, our loaded closets, our three-car garages, our home theaters. This was not so in the world of my very young childhood, the sphere of World War II. It was a world of scarcity, but you were already well-rehearsed in scarcity.

You married during the Great Depression, despite the fact that Dad had lost his job. You lived several months of your early marriage in Grandmother's wash house (Grandfather's too, now I think of it, but I never knew him because he died when I was very small) on the farm in Lehi, sharing space not only with wash tubs and wood stove, but also with the lye and animal fat that Grandmother used for making blocks of soap. Too proud, you were, to share an already overcrowded house with your parents and younger siblings. Why is this story more real to me now, Mother, than it was when I heard it as a child? Why do I think of it today when I religiously use a bar of soap to the last sliver, and then attach that pliable wet sliver to the new bar instead of relegating it to the waste can?

I remember Dad telling about your first Christmas together, your holiday in the wash house. It was Christmas Eve, and you were down to your last twenty-five cents. You had bought nothing for each other, and the prospects of doing so were mighty bleak. Then, a small evergreen tree was left as a secret gift for you and Dad, on the steps of the wash house. It changed everything. You had nothing to put on it—no baubles, lights, popcorn, or cranberries. Not even colored paper. But you had twenty-five cents, and you made a decision. Off the two of you went to the little mercantile in town, to buy decorations for your tree. The merc had but one ornament left, a red pendant with gold trim. The storekeeper would sell it to you for twenty-five cents. How well I remember that ornament, gradually fading over the years, but always atop our childhood trees. The place of honor. When you and Dad died ten years ago, I found that ornament and claimed and cherished it. Somehow, in my last move, however, it was broken. I console myself with the fact that although the tangible relic is shattered, the memory is intact still, and ever will be.

But I digress, Mother (you'll get used to it, trust me). I meant to talk about the war and the extreme shortages it brought as civilian goods and manufacturing were diverted to military needs. I was old enough to realize that nearly everything we deemed essential to everyday living was rationed. I can still remember the booklets of stamps and the little brown disks that allowed you to buy strictly limited amounts of foods like meat, sugar, and butter. Steel, rubber, and leather goods, as well as gasoline, were especially scarce, often non-existent.

When shoes wore out, there were none to replace them. Luckily, over the years, you had saved a supply of thin cardboard shirt stiffeners from the laundry where Dad worked, and those came in handy for children whose shoes had holes in the soles. There was no satisfactory half-sole material that would stay put on the bottom of a child's shoes, but we had those shirt boards. I remember cutting insoles from that thin cardboard to slip inside my shoes. At least for a short time, they gave my feet and socks a little protection. Sandals for children, in my childhood world anyway, were unheard of, so we always played and went to school in shoes and socks. Incidentally, darning socks, you recall, was a weekly chore, one that fell to me when I was old enough to wield a fat needle. Nylon reinforced heels and toes had not been invented yet, and no one in our house dreamed of discarding a sock until it was past repair.

Since food, along with everything else, was in short supply, Americans were encouraged to plant "victory gardens."

Bittersweet

True, we had a weed patch behind our house that was not employed to any useful purpose, though mosquitoes and grasshoppers seemed to enjoy it. You, Mother, determined that we were going to buy seeds and plant a garden there, just beyond the lawn. Which is what we did, without bringing in any topsoil or fertilizer. We learned from this little experiment that it is one thing to plant seeds and quite another to reap a harvest, especially in what was possibly the rockiest soil this side of Mars.

Yes, a few plants actually sprouted and even grew roots vaguely resembling radishes and carrots beneath their greenish tops. These sorry-looking vegetables were worse for the wear (your expression) as they contended for space with the rocks that seemed to multiply daily. The more rocks we tossed out, the more rocks appeared to take their places. Consequently, our radishes were dented and blemished, and our carrots were pathetic orange corkscrews. Still, we faithfully choked a few down, as a show of patriotism and in support of you, Mother. (Did you threaten us? No. Threats were not your style.)

Enough about war and thrift, at least for now. I suspect thrift will resurface again, it being such a defining factor in our life together, and in our life apart. Recent events have dictated a shift in focus at this point, Mother. Forgive the following digression.

Marilyn in a red velveteen coat and bonnet.

Upper right: Rhoda holding baby Marilyn on porch steps. Below, Marilyn in "jammies" made by Mother, and (right) with Dad, again in the red velveteen coat and bonnet made by Mother.

Marilyn with her "blue" birthday cake.

Ned and Marilyn in front of their Ogden home, both in "jammies" made by Mother.

Marilyn Arnold

Rhoda with Rey and Marilyn, and Rey, Ned, and Marilyn. Below: Marilyn, Ned, and Rey with the family's 1936 Plymouth.

Page Three
(An Interlude, a Page We Don't Share)

Thursday evening, Mother, your firstborn son passed away. He, my older brother, though really not so much older, died, left us here wringing our hands and our hearts. But then, I guess you knew that even before I did. My faith tells me that he has joined you and Dad, and that you probably attended his passing. My faith also tells me that his collapsed body is no longer a hindrance, a drag on his spirit, and that he has entered a new era of running marathons in the sky. (He told me not long ago that sometimes in his dreams he was running, joyfully, freely running as he used to.) My faith assures me that I will see him again in a brighter world, a world free of the plagues of sickness, hatred, and wars—though I wonder about war, considering that the first great war was, after all, fought in heaven.

My faith, however, does not stop the tears and sleepless nights beset with sorrow and loss. He, that once powerful running machine, was addicted to tobacco, and in the end it won the race, killing him slowly but not softly. In the end, wracked by emphysema, he was reduced to skin and bones, his lungs virtually destroyed. In the end, pneumonia overtook him, and the oxygen tubes that had become his umbilical cord of life could no longer sustain him. He made the decision, Mother, to let go, as I suspect you did a decade earlier.

I had known for a long time that one day, one day, the dire call would come. I had wanted to postpone it forever. Thursday afternoon, February 28, it came, around three o'clock. "Marilyn," he said, in a voice strained with effort and grief, though decisive and tender. "Marilyn, this is the hardest call I have ever had to make." And then he told me that the doctors held out no hope and that everything in his body was shutting down. He called to say goodbye, Mother, and to say that he loved me and that he knew we would meet again in the next life. He called to say that he was removing the oxygen tubes. (I learned later, however, that he went to sleep with the tubes still in place, still streaming oxygen into his nostrils. He went to sleep, and then he went quietly to death.) He said not to come (to Yuma, Arizona, where he and his spouse had gone in January, to avoid northern Utah's winter viruses and bacteria, an irony not lost on me), that he would lapse into unconsciousness very quickly and be gone in two or three days. Well, Mother, he was gone in two or three hours.

Bittersweet

    I think I wept myself dry that afternoon and night. I hadn't felt so grief-stricken since you died, Mother, and all of that inconsolable ache came back to me. Dad's passing, a month after yours, was different. He could not have survived without you, his mind being mostly gone, and he suffered convulsions and a coma the day after we buried you. His life was over and his passing a blessing. But your death, Mother, came unexpectedly, though your life was a struggle those last years. You probably didn't know of the poet May Swenson, but she said that when her mother died, she knew she had experienced the worst thing that would ever happen to her. That's how I felt when you died, Mother, as if nothing else could produce such agony again. But I was wrong. The death of a beloved sibling can benumb and devastate in a way that I hadn't imagined possible.

    Is it because I have no husband or children? Is that why these deaths hit me so hard? Or does everyone feel this way at the loss of a dear one? Does everyone weep for hours and then move about in a stupor for days, even weeks? I had to do something after those fateful calls, one then the other, just hours apart, but I didn't know what. So I walked, then I polished my car, and then I began cleaning my house. I don't mind polishing a car, but I hate housecleaning. I did it anyway. It might have helped a little, and it filled up Friday and part of Saturday. I was reminded of an Emily Dickinson poem that calls this kind of domestic "bustle" after a death "the solemnest" of earthly "industries." It is a figurative "sweeping up" of the heart, a "putting away" of love until we "need" it again in eternity. Emily knew, oh yes, she knew. The hard way.

I remember now that I also went to work like there was no tomorrow, in your home, Mother, after your death. It was all I could do. I remember that the younger neighbors who came by seemed alarmed at my apparent callousness, alarmed that I went to sorting and packing and cleaning out your house even before the funeral. They didn't understand that industry under such circumstances is a way of dealing with grief. Keep the body busy to keep the emotions in check. After terrible loss, one has to do *something*. Something that keeps the mind and heart at bay. The older ones understood. They had known loss and heart-wrenching sorrow.

Well, Mother, I am back home again. The funeral for your firstborn son was Saturday, in a Church meetinghouse near his home, nine days after his passing. It was a long nine days. Many fine tributes were paid him, and your sibling's children, my cousins, turned out in force, as they always do. Two of the three remaining cousins on Dad's side of the family came also. And of course, your two youngest sisters, my only living aunts. Your lastborn son spoke wonderfully, tenderly, at the services, as we all knew he would. And your

Bittersweet

granddaughter and grandsons spoke lovingly and memorably of their father.

There was no casket, no body, no satin, no stiff limbs, no powdery face. Your son had asked that his remains be given to science, that lessons might be learned from his mistakes. There will be ashes at some point, after the tissue harvest. Those ashes your grandsons had thought to scatter outside the rustic mountain cabin where the family laughed and played and talked together through many happy summers and hunting seasons. But then they thought better of it and decided to bury the ashes beneath a headstone in a small cemetery, a place of enduring comfort for them and their mother.

Formalities. The seams that keep us from splitting apart, flying to pieces. A mountain cabin is a formality. A campfire is a formality. A funeral is a formality. A note, a phone call, a hug, a flower, a song—each is a formality. So is holding back, protecting loved ones from our sorrow. So is letting go in the solemn aloneness of our private grief. Even memory is a formality. So is writing about love and loss, and about memory itself. Every day, Mother, I still think of you and miss you. Does that surprise you? I think it surprises me to realize finally that it will ever be so, every day of my life, every day between your death and my own.

My chief consolation at this moment, aside from my faith in the atoning power of Jesus Christ, is the assurance that your lastborn son will outlast me, that I will not have to survive and endure his mortal death. He is my mortal rock. He and his wife. He and his sons, who have been as my own. Your firstborn's sons and daughter are dear, but we have not shared very much of our lives. They are good and kind, but always exclusively their father's and mother's, now hers more than ever. Still she and I are good friends and will always be friends.

I came home yesterday, in time to catch the late service at church and to stumble through choir rehearsal. Then, compliments of daylight saving time, which began yesterday, I changed into walking clothes and sought the cleansing of sand and sandstone and lava rock under my feet. It wasn't until I turned around on Mustang Pass and began the gentle descent that the desert began to have its way with me, began to soothe my soul. Maybe it was the horizontal slant of the lowering sun lighting up the eastern bluffs, or the light breeze ruffling my hair, that made the difference.

You never knew the desert, Mother, never knew its healing power. Oh, you had passed through it a few times, but it had never become yours. And you didn't understand the gut-deep need in me for its sparse, magnificent beauty. You never scrambled up a red rock crevice, or slogged a bright stream between high rugged walls, or maneuvered your way up a boulder-filled wash, or came unexpectedly on a high

Bittersweet

sandstone arch carving a chunk out of the bluest sky on earth. You never marveled at vast acres of cactus in bloom, or wind-swirled rock in layers of red, yellow, and ivory. You never rejoiced at the cascading song of a canyon wren, or rushing water slithering through sculptured rock.

You had your joys, however, even before the advent of grandchildren, in fourth and fifth grade classrooms where you changed lives one at a time, where you lighted flames in young minds and tamed souls seemingly destined for self-destruction. You never knew the thrill of racing down snow-covered mountains with narrow boards attached to your feet, or climbing a mountain and shooting wildly down a huge, steep glacier on the back side of your cutoff jeans, or rappelling off the Grand Teton. (Of course, you never wore jeans at all, much less cut-offs. When you finally ventured out of "house dresses" and into slacks, you went straight to elastic top polyester.) Your pleasures were tamer ones than mine, Mother, though we both loved books and cherry trees in bloom and red, red roses.

In all fairness to you, Mother, you came to accept the fact that you hadn't given birth to the conventional daughter you expected. I think you decided, finally, that perhaps I was more interesting (at least more perplexing and challenging!) than a more conventional daughter would have been. And yes, you took pride in what you regarded as my "accomplishments." And I suspect that you may even have boasted just a little about your children (in your understated way) to your sisters and perhaps a neighbor or two. As I seem to keep saying, I never doubted that I loved you. I never doubted that you loved me. Never. It would not have occurred to me. And your sons. Oh, how you loved your sons. But we never had to compete for your love. There was plenty to go around.

Enough of this for now, Mother. Return with me to childhood. We were talking about thrift, weren't we? But that was not the dominant factor in my early life with you. I have many lovely memories, many pages to share. Let's go to some of them now, though the possibility always exists that I will get sidetracked again.

Dad and Mother at our Ogden home.

Bittersweet

Ned's and Rey's families, with Marilyn, Mother, and Dad.

Marilyn Arnold

Rey's "gang," including his daughter, Tawni, and her family (left) from Alaska.

Page Four

You, Mother, were a woman of sayings—you know, catch phrases appropriate to a given moment. They were all so "you" philosophically, and were intended to be instructive to your children. There was scarcely a situation for which you had no ready phrase. Sometimes you came out with a standard proverbial adage such as "waste not, want not," or "a penny saved is a penny earned," but more often your utterances were original with either you or your forebears. I don't recall hearing sayings like yours from Grandmother, however. They come to mind in odd, unexpected moments.

Those bits of folk wisdom seem to be afloat in my brain, not to be called up on demand, but only to be plucked out when something triggers a memory. One such occurs to me just now. If as a youngster I was carrying on about something of minor importance (in your scale of values), making far too much of it—for instance, wailing, "I can't go out with my hair looking like this!"— you would say calmly, "It will never be seen on a galloping horse." On the other hand, if I were minimizing something that you regarded as important, you would say, "It's an awful lot on the end of your nose."

Two statements I heard frequently as a child. The first was in code, "C.O.B.I." It was a code that possibly only your children in all the world understood. It meant "Chest out, belly in." In other words, "Stand up straight (or sit up straight), child. Don't slump." The second was "Close your mouth and breathe through your nose." No code involved there. It was about as direct as an instruction could be. You did not want your children going around with their mouths hanging open.

Well, Mother, I got the message even as a tiny tot. You liked to tell of the day when you and I were in downtown Ogden, waiting for the light to change so that we could cross Washington Boulevard. I was three years old. At that same crossing sat a very large dog, on his haunches, panting and dripping saliva from his very long tongue. I (so your story goes) went up to the dog, put my arm around his neck, and admonished him in your voice: "Close your mouth and breathe through your nose." So you see, Mother, you had quite an impact on your daughter from the beginning.

One of my favorites of your sayings, and one of your most memorable, was another comment that only a member of your household would understand. This cryptic response came out of your mouth when you learned something you hadn't known before: "Well, I can go to bed now." The statement grew out of one of your repeated injunctions to your children: "Don't go to bed until you have learned something new." Yes, indeed, you began honing your children's brains early. Learning and teaching were the staples of your life. We never heard the phrase "*if* you go to college" from either you or Dad. It was always "*when* you go to college." And we were expected to qualify for scholarships, too, because the family budget and our own earnings could not stretch across tuition as well as living expenses and books.

A side note here. You remember, Mother, that your children always worked to earn money, summers and after school (and after spring cleaning!), from the time we were big enough to pick fruit or weed onions. Children like us were the "migrant workers" of those days. There was even a bus that came through town hauling young pickers out to the orchards in North Ogden. My older brother also delivered newspapers on his bicycle, riding nine miles every day, winter and summer, up and down hilly streets; and all of us had our turns at hard labor in the laundry, which was not air-conditioned. I remember when I ascended from menial work to waiting on customers in the front office. That job paid sixty cents an hour, and I thought I was on easy street. Then, when I became a student at BYU and landed a job after school and summers as a cub reporter for the *Deseret News*, I knew I had hit the gravy train. (And somewhere along the way, while in junior college in Ogden, I worked at the YWCA with the youth program, at the Catholic High School as a part-time gym teacher, and at Grand Canyon.)

In addition to being a woman of many sayings you were also a gifted storyteller, Mother, and you needed no script. The stories were all in your head, word for word, planted there by your mother, and by her mother before her. And even though I can't repeat them word for word the way I could as a child, your stories are in my head, too, and never as print on a page. No, I hear your voice—warm, inviting, practiced—speaking the words, inflecting in all the right places and swinging in the expressive rhythm only you could give a sentence. They were stories I never heard or encountered any other place—not in books, not in school, not in libraries. It was as if they were part of the equipment you were born with, as if they were stamped in your DNA.

Where, for example, did the story of Lambikin (would you have spelled it "Lammikin"?) and Drummikin ("Drumikin"?) originate? No other voice could utter these words like yours, in the most appealing sing-song fashion: "He's fallen in the river, and you'll fall, too. Come little Lambikin, tumpy-tump, tooo—tumpy-tump tooo." Until this moment, I had never seen those words written, and I doubt

Bittersweet

that you ever did either. Again, how would you have spelled them if called upon, you who could spell anything and who never dropped a verbal "g" from a single -ing ending in your life. I can still hear you correcting me when I committed the unpardonable by saying something like, "I'm comin'." Through a loving frown you would say, "Don't be a "g" dropper, Marilyn." Even now I feel a twinge of guilt when I carelessly drop a "g." I confess, Mother, that no longer having a "g" dropper inhabiting the White House is a great relief to me. Being your daughter, I'm certain that I suffered more than most people through two terms of publicly dropped "g's." My ears have welcomed the respite.

Another story I remember was about Mother West Wind and her seven little breezes. True, my research has uncovered a series of Mother West Wind stories by Thornton W. Burgess, none of which even vaguely resembles your story, Mother. Yours, I suspect, came through a long line of oral tellers who took Burgess's original notion and created a new plot and character. I am sorely tempted to repeat the story here, Mother, as you once recorded it for me on tape. It is about the wicked Green Goblin who approaches the home of Mother West Wind after she has gone off to work (a working mother, way back then—one with seven children, no less!), blowing fishing boats out in the morning and back to port in the evening.

In a series of magical transformations originally intended

to fool the little breezes into admitting him into their home for purposes of mischief, the Goblin ultimately becomes a good and trusted friend. I can still hear you delivering the repeated phrases, with childlike verve, each time the Goblin appears at the door, "Oh, you look like our friend. Open the door! Open the door!" Six of the little breezes are easily fooled, but the cautious little breeze always submits the Goblin to one more test that reveals his evil nature. Gradually his appearance is changed, and then his voice. In the end, even his nature is changed.

Thus, while affirming that there is wisdom in caution, your story taught us (and your grandchildren) that even bad people can change and become good if, as your story says, they "really want to," and they "work really hard" at it. You always filled your stories with high drama, Mother, whether you were telling about the Trolls under the bridge who threatened Lambikin and Drummikin, or the wicked Green Goblin, or whether you were reciting your version of "The Pig Brother" to teach us the importance of cleanliness and good grooming. No self-respecting animal in the barnyard (except the pig!) would associate with young John, who had left the house without washing his hands and face and combing his hair. You were full of *exempla*, always teaching, teaching, teaching, even when we thought you were merely entertaining us. Looking back, I can see that we should have known better. You never passed up an opportunity to instruct children, especially

Bittersweet

your own. (No wonder you were kept as Junior Sunday School coordinator in our ward for twenty years.)

Your repertoire, Mother, included poems as well as stories. And you told them word for word, inflection for inflection, the same every time, just as with your stories. I remember in particular "Two Little Kittens" ("Two little kittens one stormy night, began to quarrel and then to fight . . ."). One of your great-granddaughters recited the latter for me at age three or four, so your legacy lives on. Most of your poems, like your stories, I have never encountered elsewhere. "Little Orphan Annie," however, which you learned from your mother, can be traced to an author outside the family. But like every story and poem that rolled off your tongue, it carries a message especially for children. If you talk back to adults, or make fun of others, or fail to say your prayers, Orphan Annie warns, "the goblins'll get you if you don't watch out!" (Earlier generations seemed to have a thing about goblins!)

As far as I know, you never committed a single story or poem to paper. They were all inscribed on the pages of your incredible mind. That same mind served you well when you could no longer see more than shapes and shadows. You memorized dozens of phone numbers and other vital facts and information, including the account numbers of your certificates of deposit. When your signature was required on a document, I guided your hand to the proper place on the page, and then you slowly penned each letter of your name.

You loved riddles and puzzles, Mother. Anything that challenged your mind. You wanted to teach children in a formal way, as well as informally at home, and you wanted to be fully credentialed; so you went back to school. You had a two-year certificate, which is all that was required for teaching when you went to college. And with your experience, you could have continued teaching without additional schooling. But you wanted that four-year degree, and by golly you got it. We were all there at your commencement exercises, Dad bursting with pride and you bursting with relief.

In those days, I didn't begin to appreciate what it cost you to teach fourth graders all day, then take extension classes and study at night. It seems you were always taking classes, winter and summer. I can still see you at the kitchen table (our only "desk") studying into the night as the rest of us went off to bed. It occurs to me now to ask, where did I study in those years and beyond? Oddly enough, I have no recollection of my own study and class preparation, but only of yours. Why did your study impress me more than my own?

I even remember sitting beside you, or on the floor at your feet, my back against your chair or a table leg or a door, quizzing you for an upcoming exam. Those times were

Bittersweet

something of a replay of early childhood when we children sat cross-legged at your feet, sometimes rubbing them just to feel close and loved, while you read to us. I remember that you took a required art class, Mother, and that I was young enough to be very impressed by what seemed to me a magnificent comical cow which you (my very own mother!) produced on drawing paper in living color—with pastels, I believe.

Still vivid in my mind's eye is that silly cow's face turned toward me in its frame of curly horns. If I remember right, it was a creamy, yellowish cow, and I thought it the finest cow I had ever seen. What else you might have drawn made no lasting impression on my child self, but that cow convinced me that you had untapped artistic abilities. I knew then, if I had not known before, that you were wonderful. Now I think of it, whatever happened to that cow, Mother? How I wish I had claimed it before it disappeared into some undeserving trash bin.

Amazingly, although I can remember the subject of no paper I myself wrote at any time before the last years of graduate school—not in junior high, high school, undergraduate college, or most of graduate school—I remember a fine research paper you wrote on Eskimo children. How is it that I remember such a thing? And now that I think of it, I can remember the subject of only one of my own graduate papers (John Milton's *Paradise Lost*) and of scarcely any published articles throughout my professorial career and since (and there have been *a lot*, Mother).

Today they seem to have little to do with me, with the person I am now. An emeritus professor—a novelist, I suppose you could call me—and a semi-scholarly essayist. And a desert rat (and erstwhile tennis bum), through and through. We never talked of writers like Flannery O'Connor, or Walker Percy, or John Milton, you and I, and we should have. True believers, they. Why didn't I read passages of *Paradise Lost* to you? You would have marveled at Milton's powerfully detailed portrayal of the pre-existence, the Creation, the Son's volunteering to die for man, the casting out of Lucifer, the great war in heaven, the reconciliation of Adam and Eve to their loss of Eden. Was it my fault (for not offering) or yours (for not asking) that we didn't share such things?

Granted, before your eyes failed you, you read Willa Cather's novels and liked them. But did we ever really discuss them? I don't remember that we did. And her work was what I knew best and wrote of most in my professorial years. (Why didn't I offer to let you read some of my papers and articles, or peruse my books on her works? What was the matter with me? Why did I, hardly the shy type, sidestep such things?)

In any case, my desires changed, Mother, as did both my interior life and my exterior life, when I at last delved head-

Bittersweet

long (and heart first) into the *Book of Mormon*, studying it closely, making it my own, giving it the careful attention I had previously invested only in exceptional literary texts. Everything in the workaday world faded in significance when I gave myself to that miracle of a book. You, Mother, did no less. Before your eyesight fled almost totally, you read a large print edition again and again. (And now, with deepening wonder, I have collaborated with a gifted friend on a book of thirty-two original hymns based on the *Book of Mormon*.)

That book of inspired scripture created a bond between you and me in the last years of your life, a bond we felt but didn't express verbally. Still, we knew it was there, more than we knew most things about each other. Through the generosity of a neighbor with a willing voice, you were able to hear my book-length commentary on the *Book of Mormon*, titled *Sweet Is the Word*. (I should have read it to you myself, but didn't. Again, I failed you.)

But I digress. As usual. In this particular page of our lives I meant to speak only of my childhood years with you, Mother, but I keep leaving those years and leaping into the more recent past. Let me return now to that older past and the stories that so define it for me. I began this chapter with a remembrance of your remarkable gift as a storyteller, a gift I took for granted as a child. In fact, I came to appreciate your achievement fully only as an adult, when I myself became an inventor of tales rather than merely a traveler in stories told or written by others. And now it is too late to tell you how wonderful you were as you spun your word magic with tales that spoke to every child's heart. Why didn't I praise you to the skies? Why didn't I bring others to hear you? Why didn't I play your recorded stories in my university classes? (You would never have come in person. Strong as you were in will and integrity, you were reticent before any audience except one composed of young children.)

Your stories, Mother, were not limited to delightful fictions for the youthful imagination. You also told my brothers and me stories of your own childhood in rural Lehi; and as children we begged to hear them over and over, just as we begged to hear about the Green Goblin and Lambikin. It was the very personal stories, those specific to you, that we wanted most to hear. There were funny ones, mysterious ones, and frightening ones; and we loved them all. I was relieved to learn that you were not a perfect child, that you were capable of participating in, and even initiating, a little (not entirely innocent) deception. Looking back now at the evasions of our protective mother-daughter dance, I realize yet again how much I loved those sweet early days when candor graced our relationship.

Bittersweet

The day you almost started school. Now there's a story. Even now I hear you chuckling to tell how on the first day of school, at age five, you were scrubbed and dressed by your older sisters for your first grade debut. There was a problem, however: you would not be officially eligible until you turned six in January, and kindergarten and pre-school had not been invented yet. The preparations were done clandestinely so that your mother (a straighter arrow never lived) would not know the plan to start you in first grade before school policy allowed.

The girls slipped you out of the house and down the lane to walk the two miles with them to the little country school house. But, excited as you were to be starting school with the big kids, your conscience got the best of you. You looked back (when you allowed as how you had reached the point of no return) and called in the loudest voice you could muster, "Mother, goodbye. I'm going to school!" And then you ran ahead, just to play it safe. It was quite a scheme, Mother, but it didn't work. You were not allowed to enroll until a year later. You got your revenge, however. You skipped the fourth grade—ironically, the very grade you would teach most of your life. I think it safe to say that you mastered the material.

Marilyn Arnold

Perhaps my favorite of your childhood stories is the trick you played on the owner of the tiny grocery store which you passed daily on your way to grade school. He was no stranger to the barter system because farm people often brought home grown or homemade items to exchange for merchandise. In fact, your mother sometimes sent eggs from her chickens to exchange for some item she needed. Thus it was that the proprietor didn't question you when you appeared with an egg in hand and asked for a certain candy bar. One thing was amiss, however: you failed to mention to the trusting merchant that the egg was not fresh, but hard-boiled! You laughed to tell us that it didn't occur to you that someone might have purchased that egg with the intention of baking a cake. All you knew was that you had a hankering for a candy bar, and there was an uninspiring hard-boiled egg in your lunch box. I have to say, Mother, that you were a very resourceful child.

By the way, Mother, that tiny devious streak showed itself at least once in your mother role, too. Laughing guiltily, you confessed to your middle-aged daughter your secret for bed-wetting prevention in small children. We were given nothing to drink after 6 p.m. If we were thirsty, you gave us only a tiny sip of water, thus assuring that our bladders would not overflow during the night. As we laughed together over your trick, I accused you of "cruelty to dumb animals."

How I love those early stories about you, Mother, you

Bittersweet

who were (nearly) always so proper in your mother role. I can't help wondering about other possible stories that you didn't tell. One story that I shuddered to hear, however, was about the day your clothing caught fire during soap-making activities on the farm. Apparently, despite your mother's warnings, you bent too close to the burning coals. Terrified, you ran while the flames licked up your legs. Your older brother chased you down and rolled you in the dirt to smother the flames. What if he hadn't been nearby?

I remember my stomach turning when you showed me the scarring on the insides of your legs. I couldn't bear to think of you injured and in great pain, ever. And still can't. Why have I needed you to be indomitable, indestructible, beyond mortal hurt? Why couldn't I allow you to be human, vulnerable, wounded? Was this my personal flaw, or do other daughters encase their mothers in an invincible shield so that, for as long as possible, they do not have to see their mothers anguish or danger?

And then there was the mysterious event when it seemed your life was inexplicably, perhaps miraculously, spared. You told of a fierce thunderstorm that struck when you were at the home of a playmate. Power lines and pole came down in the front yard of the farmhouse, and you went running out barefooted to see. (Were you trying to save your shoes from water damage—and yourself from reprimand, Mother—or was there a time when you relished running shoeless in wet grass, savoring its sweet, tickling massage? I'd like to think it was the latter, but experience tells me it was probably the former.)

The lines were still alive, strewn across the rain-soaked grass. You stepped on the tangled wires, Mother, and were slammed to the ground across the wires, apparently unconscious. Your friend went screaming into the house, and when her parents came rushing, you were gone. A search of the premises revealed you sitting calmly on the back steps of the house, unhurt. You had no idea how you got off the wires and around the house. You suffered no ill effects from the incident, except a lengthy lecture from your father. (You always spoke of him as "Father," never "Papa" or "Daddy" or "Dad." I always thought that a bit formal because we children never called Dad "Father," and we don't speak of him that way even now.)

There was another mysterious event that you told us about, Mother. You were in your teens, walking on a street in downtown Lehi with two school friends. (Calling it "downtown" in those days may have been something of a stretch, but there were apparently a few shops in a row.) A stranger, a woman unknown to any of you, approached and called you aside. In private she indicated that you had a special destiny for which you should prepare yourself, though she didn't specify what that destiny was. You were both puzzled and

Bittersweet

frightened by the encounter and quickly rejoined your friends. When you turned back for a second look at the woman, she was gone. You tried to find her but she had disappeared as though into thin air. You never saw her again, nor did anyone to whom you described her recognize her. Her clothing and manner struck you as odd, somehow characteristic of another time and place.

No such events have ever happened to me, Mother, but those inscrutable experiences of yours have staked claims in the pages of my mind. They surface every now and then, like allergies in April, or a mysterious rash on the back or the face, one that comes and goes without explaining itself. Having reminisced a bit in your early past, I propose we leave it and turn to a happy event in your somewhat later past, an event you and Dad shared with us at the supper table one evening. Oh yes, we always had supper together, home-cooked from scratch, unless you were in class during our regular dinner hour.

If there were pizza parlors in those days, we never knew it. Even after the war, when meat was no longer rationed, you still saw no reason to go out for a hamburger when we could make a better one at home for less money—with ground round steak, too, rather than the fattier burgers sold at the A & W. On your school nights I cooked, for better or worse, and the men of the family endured. (I suspect that Dad threatened the boys with unending KP duty, or worse, if they uttered a word of complaint or failed to clean their plates.)

But back to the supper table story. I have to say, Mother, that I could never have pictured you as a "vamp." Still, unless your pictures lie, you were nothing short of drop dead gorgeous—modest gorgeous, yes, but gorgeous nonetheless. No wonder a certain young man was smitten when you arrived as the new school marm in the little company mining town of Lark, Utah, one early September day. The problem was that particular young man was engaged to another young woman at the time, a woman who was away from home just then and unable to defend her territorial rights to the young man who would become our father.

You, Mother, thought you had arrived at the end of the earth. (Incidentally, Mother, the town of your early dismay has since been completely dismantled and bulldozed, wiped off the map by executive fiat.) Dad happened to see you, weeping in despair outside the boarding house where you were to lodge. Being the chivalrous sort, naturally he felt compelled to approach and offer assistance. And being a helpless maiden in distress, you gladly accepted his gallant offering of solace. Naturally, the townsfolk did not approve of this unexpected liaison, at least not until they got used to the idea.

Their loyalty was with the absent lady love who was, after all, one of them and not a stranger. Small town people tend not to trust strangers, not even school teacher strangers. (Maybe *especially* not beautiful young school teacher strangers.)

Well, needless to say, Dad's absentee lady love didn't stand a chance from that day on. He courted you as only a small-town boy could court a lonesome young woman who had arrived, seemingly dropped down from heaven, into his grassless world of mining folk, dirt streets, and scarcely water enough for drinking, much less for plumbing. And he won you. How well I remember that night at supper when Dad told the story of your meeting and courtship in detail only hinted at before, embellishing it shamelessly for our benefit. How my brothers and I laughed! I think you and Dad laughed so hard you nearly tumbled off your chairs. Tears of merriment ran down your cheeks, Mother, as you defended your innocence while we merrily accused you of being a home-wrecker, of stealing Dad from his promised lady love by feigning utter helplessness and homesickness.

That night around our little drop-leaf kitchen table was magic, filled with a beauty that I shall never forget. It was the essence of family togetherness. In a lifetime, there are precious few moments like that, moments of pure happiness. Not that you were a gloomy person, Mother—you weren't at all—but that's the only time I saw you laugh until you couldn't speak. I think it was my first experience of unabashed joy, a joy born out of love and simple delight in being part of a family.

Marilyn Arnold

"Aunt Marilyn" with Rey's three boys, Rod, Chad, and Joe. Five-year-old Joe went on the 1977 "Mud" trip described in a later chapter.

Page Five

Memories are flooding my mind, Mother, memories of my childhood in your home. They have no logical order because, like dreams or loose pages cast into the wind, memory is neither logical nor sequential. It seems I have to take these memories as they come. They pop up of their own will, and perhaps the crazy quilt pattern they create has its own order, its own formality, not to be disputed. As I indicated before, Mother, you were not athletic to even the tiniest degree. Come to think of it, I never remember seeing you throw a ball, skip a rock in the river (or toss one at a stray dog), ride a bicycle, jump rope, or participate in anything resembling a sport. But as I also said earlier, you were a loyal fan, so long as the team wore BYU blue.

This does not mean you were inactive, however. No couch potato you. As a youngster, you worked hard on your father's farm and in your mother's coal-stove kitchen, where canning fruit and vegetables and making bread were a major means of subsistence for a big family. As an adult non-driver, walking is what you did—and gardening, and cooking, and canning, and house cleaning with a vengeance.

You never showed your hand by playing catch with us, or trying to hit a ball with a real bat. You did, however, when we pushed you in the matter of athleticism, claim to be a good runner. On our occasional family picnics in the park, you would agree to race with us, from one tree to another. (Dad never condescended.) So long as we were small you won handily although you ran "like a girl," as we used to say. But the years passed, and one day your firstborn son reached the designated finish line ahead of you. That was the day your career as a sprinter ended. We could never cajole you into racing us again.

You were not what anyone would consider "laid back," but you did have one casual piece of attire in those days (i.e., something with pant legs) for picnics and outings, a one-piece, short-sleeved cotton jump suit that nipped in neatly at the waist. In my mind I see you racing ahead of me through the grass in that outfit, which seemed so right for you. I suppose you could call it faded mauve, or "maroon chambray." Your rather nondescript house dresses from J.C. Penney's or Mode O'Day, your uniform of choice at home, blur together in my mind, along with your aprons. But for some reason, today I see you clearly in that reddish outfit, smiling radiantly at our old Brownie camera, bandanna tied fetchingly

Bittersweet

through your wavy, dark brown hair. I think I also see Dad, his arm locked in yours, posing for a picture. Did I know then how beautiful you were? I don't think it even occurred to me. After all, you were just "Mother."

We didn't vacation much, Mother, but when we did, I think you wore that outfit. Money was scarce and Dad never seemed to get much time off work. The two or three vacations we took together are very dim in my memory. Which should prove something about what makes a lasting impression on children. I think there was one trip to the redwoods (in our 1936 Plymouth) where we drove through a tree tunnel, and another where we wound up in some flea-bitten motel in the Nevada or Utah boondocks because Dad was too tired to drive any farther. I remember that you were not happy with the lumpy beds, the dark outhouse, the old wash basin and pitcher. But that's all I remember. I don't know where we were or where we had been or where we were going. I only remember that you did not want to stop at such a place and Dad insisted. Your displeasure and Dad's insistence in the face of it is the only thing that stayed in my memory. Isn't that interesting? I couldn't bear for you and Dad to be at odds over anything, ever. I couldn't bear for us to be anything but happy together.

Marilyn Arnold

With few exceptions, my childhood memories are happy ones. Those were the days when I scarcely thought beyond the next birthday party, mine or someone else's. Those parties were not elaborate affairs. The games consisted of such thrillers as pin-the-tail-on-the-donkey (a home-drawn one) or blind-man's-bluff (I think we used to call it "Buff") or musical chairs, followed by the opening of equally thrilling gifts—typically hair ribbons, coloring books, crayons, or jars of bubble-blowing fluid—and the serving of birthday cake, one piece of which might contain a baked-in dime for a prize.

I remember that one year when I was very small, I insisted on a *blue* cake and blue frosting. (I somehow became aware that cakes could be made pink or blue with tiny drops of mysterious fluid kept in small, thin bottles in our cupboard.) You indulged me, Mother, against your better judgment, and the cake was a disaster. It *tasted* blue, and blue did not taste good. My young taste buds could not get past the message coming from my eyes. Much as you hated to do it, you (or was it Dad?) threw the cake out. If I remember right, we did not have cake again for a good long time. You made your point.

Desserts were rare in our house in any case. Except on birthdays, they were exclusively Sunday events. Weekdays we made do with home-canned fruit or jello, which often had the stuff of salad in it, and therefore in the opinion of the children of the house, did not qualify as dessert. Contrary to your view of things, in my mind fruit cocktail or bananas in the mix were better than cabbage, but still did not make jello a legitimate dessert (children's rule number one: nothing that can be considered remotely *good for you* can qualify as dessert). Even a dab of whipped cream on top did not really qualify it in our minds, though we knew it was intended to placate us. And speaking of whipped cream, Mother, you never squandered good money on whipping cream in its own container unless we had company, and then you bought only half-pints and made the delicacy stretch. (I was thirteen, at least, before I learned that whipping cream also came in *pint* containers.)

In those days, milk was not homogenized, but arrived on the front porch in quart bottles with the cream visible in a band at the top. (I never understood how the thicker and seemingly weightier cream stayed afloat on the seemingly less weighty milk.) Carefully, you poured the risen cream into a bowl and whipped it with a hand beater. Whipping the cream, and adding sugar and vanilla, became my job when I was big enough to take it on. I liked that job because I got to lick the beaters and the bowl when the work was finished. If we had heard of calories and saturated fat in those days (and I seriously doubt it), we paid no attention. Little did I know that I was regularly drinking skimmed milk even as a child (which should add *years* to my life, if there is any justice).

Marilyn Arnold

Maybe we didn't get chubby because there were fewer things to tempt us then (or because we drank skimmed milk!). The aftermath of the Great Depression and World War II did not train us in gluttony. We were reared on scarcity. Halloween, Christmas, and Easter candy had to last us all year, so we children hoarded it like little squirrels. I remember standing in line at the miniscule store next to my elementary school, a penny or two clutched in my fist, hoping to be one of the blessed few to get one or two pieces of genuine Fleer's Double Bubble Gum when a batch came in. Not only did each piece (which could be halved and thus prolonged) come wrapped in a little comic strip, but it was the only bubble gum worthy of the name, and it was mighty scarce during the war. The stuff that was regularly available tasted and chewed like pink wallpaper cleaner, and it made inferior bubbles. (I still remember the day the war ended. We children ran outside to celebrate with the neighborhood, yelling and cheering, turning somersaults and dancing on Ingebretsens' lawn.)

I confess now, for the first time, to sneaking Nestle's chocolate chips from the bag you kept hidden away for special cookie occasions, Mother (after the war, of course, when such delicacies again became available). Even then, you always divided the bag and used only half the semi-sweet

Bittersweet

morsels for a batch of cookies. (It wasn't calories you wanted to limit, but cost.) I found a way to get into an unopened bag through the back seam, using a very thin knife. If you discovered my ruse, you never let on. Perhaps you thought enterprise deserved to be rewarded. I also swiped a package of jello from your cupboard once, to lick the sweet grains out of my grubby little palm, but found it less than satisfying. Possibly there was too much dirt in the mix.

Don't get me wrong, Mother. I know that we were allowed certain special treats. Sometimes on a Saturday night in summer Dad (he was "Daddy" then) would get a hankering for an ice cream cone, and we would drive down to Farr's ice cream shop. Dad always got a double-decker, but children and mothers were expected to settle for a single, which cost a nickel. Every once in a while Dad would get a similar hankering for some home-made root beer, and the two of you would brew up a batch. (I was fascinated by the odd-shaped capping instrument that came out of the depths of the kitchen cabinet for these occasions.) Such luxuries, of course, were pre-war and post-war. During the war sugar was rationed and could not be wasted on trifling indulgences.

You would not like me to make this account sound as though we were deprived as children. Actually, we were not. We were materially deprived only by today's standards. We

Marilyn Arnold

lived pretty much like everyone else in our neighborhood and school. It never occurred to us children that we might be considered poor. All we knew was that people with money lived elsewhere, on the east bench mainly. I didn't meet any of their children until I went to high school, and they were clearly in the minority. In fact, children today seem deprived to me, deprived of the childhood freedoms we took for granted.

As I look (lovingly!) at my own grandnieces and grandnephews, I see them surrounded by toys and games and gadgets and clothing and soccer and dance and karate and food (which they are prone to diddle over or waste unless it's pizza or French fries or chicken nuggets) and computers and cell phones and wiis and big screens. But their world is more dangerous than my child world was, and therefore of necessity more confined and restricted. The young ones cannot play outside their yards without adult supervision. They cannot discover the shaded (and forbidden!) wonders of Birch Creek Hollow on their own, or roam the back alleys of their neighborhoods (in fact, there are no back alleys in their neighborhoods, a real loss for adventuresome children), or wander up to Putnams' little grocery store with a penny or a nickel burning a hole in their pockets, or trudge up to Jefferson Pond with their ice skates, or go sledding on Chase's Hill, or roller skate around the block, or catch the dime movie matinee at the Paramount on Saturday afternoons.

Bittersweet

Moreover, they are accustomed to being programmed or entertained with "things." I don't see them following the flight of a butterfly, or lying in the summer grass searching for four-leaf clovers. I don't see them examining grasshoppers and beetles, or bouncing around on home-made stilts. Nor do I see them playing cops and robbers with "rubber guns," and handmade from a small plank (cut roughly into handgrip and long barrel), strips of inner tube for ammunition, and a clothes pin for a trigger. I don't see them climbing trees, or playing softball in the street or a vacant lot, or inventing games to play outdoors at dusk.

Maybe they do some of these things, but perhaps under the watchful eyes of parents, or in a fenced or walled yard. Parents are afraid for their children, and rightfully so. You were able to let us flex our wings a little, Mother. And you were more of a worry-wart than most mothers. We weren't to leave the neighborhood without permission, but it was readily given, and we were to come when you hollered our names from the driveway. We learned to invent our own toyless games and create our own fun in an adult-free world. We filled our days (outside of school) with adventures of our own making. And if we came home with skinned knees or bloody noses, well, you patched us up and sent us on our way.

I do see those dear young children of mine (I claim them as my own just as I claimed their fathers) playing card games and reading and drawing and doing puzzles and crafts, as your children did, Mother, when confined to the house by weather, or darkness, or a tummy ache, or the chicken pox. And I see them tumbling on the floor with their daddies, laughing and squealing with delight. We never tumbled and squealed with Dad, did we Mother? I'm not sure he knew how to play. Maybe it was beneath the dignity of men of his generation, as official "heads of households," to frolic with their children.

Maybe if I had played more freely with Dad as a child, or if he had worked less, or gone off to fewer meetings, I'd have been more open with both of you when I moved into my teens. He let his hair down that one night at the supper table, but that was rare. Lighthearted spontaneity was not part of his nature, but he was a tender man just the same. I used to ride on his shoulder in my home-sewn bonnets (one of your specialties) and coats. He informed us regularly that we owed him a great debt for snaring you to be our mother. Oh, how he loved you!

And speaking of indoor activities, Mother, I remember that you sometimes played games with us. Not marbles, of course, which would have required you to get down on the floor in an unladylike manner, and which might have exposed an ineffective shooting technique. Would you have shot "fubby-knuckle"? (Where did we get such a term? A term that in our cryptic childhood lexicon referred to the inferior shooting method of the unskilled.) Outdoors, marbles were played with a circle scratched in dirt. (Do youngsters play marbles any more? Or mumblety-peg? Or jacks? Or hopscotch drawn with chalk on the sidewalk, and facilitated with an old shoe heel or a flat rock?) But indoors, we made do with square or rectangular throw rugs. Improvising was a way of life for children and nothing to complain about. The downside of marbles played indoors is that the small orbs were forever rolling under low-slung sofas and chairs which we could neither reach under nor move.

I didn't like playing for "keeps," indoors or out, because I could lose marbles that way. (I wonder what happened to my box of marbles? I treasured them, tucked there in my very own army surplus footlocker in the basement. How I'd like to run my fingers through those alluring glassy treasures today!) Sometimes you played such card games as Old Maid, Slap Jack, and Authors with us. Oh, how you pretended to hate getting the "Old Maid" card, and how we giggled if we managed to pass it off to you. You cried out and put on a great show of dismay for our entertainment, and we loved you for it.

A favorite with us was Pick-up Sticks, which we children quickly renamed "Fiddle Sticks." Who knows why, except that we heard you use that expression, Mother, in entirely unrelated contexts. You applied it to statements of questionable veracity, and occasionally found it handy as an expression of frustration. It was your version of "phooey." When I was still in grade school, I also loved to play "school," with myself as teacher, naturally. I mercilessly enlisted my younger brother and a neighbor child or two as my student victims, subjecting them to my vast learning, unorthodox testing practices, and rigid requirements. I remember conducting "school" in our dimly lighted, unfinished basement, out of a box where I hoarded the few teaching supplies I managed to acquire—pencils, eraser, tablets, tiny chalkboard and chalk, and a few books that I appropriated from an old bookcase in the basement.

These, you remember Mother, were the years before television. These were the years of innocence, when as a four-year-old I was appalled to see girls going to school in low-cut black or brown shoes. Such shoes were very unlike the white leather high-tops I wore daily and which you polished daily. I must have associated white leather high-tops with virtue, beauty, and truth. Even when television became available, and affordable to the masses, you would not have it in our home. At least not so long as there were young, impressionable minds under your tutelage. After I went off to college Dad bought a television set without your consent. It was the only time I ever saw him make a major purchase without your consent. He knew it was a risky business, but he did it. And eventually you forgave him.

We had radio, of course, and oh, how we loved the radio.

Bittersweet

I especially liked radio mysteries (even then, I was captivated by story, by narrative, it seems) "The Shadow," "Mr. District Attorney," "The Thin Man," among others. I can still hear that long, shivery laugh of the Shadow, Lamont something or other ("Cranston," was it?). Next on my list were "Fibber McGee and Molly," "Truth or Consequences," "The Life of Riley," and, a little later, "Your Hit Parade" hosted by Snooky Lanson. (How is it I remember that name, which I have probably misspelled, while I can scarcely remember the last names of casual friends?) My brothers did their listening downstairs in bed, through home-made crystal sets. I envied the special dispensation that allowed them to listen to "I Love a Mystery" when they were supposed to be asleep. I had to take my bedtime entertainments surreptitiously, reading by tiny flashlight under the covers.

And then there was Grandmother (whom we always called "Grandma," and whom I will call by that familiar name from here on), a longtime widow. Even though I remember your mother well, one memory stands out far above the rest: sleeping with Grandma! I didn't see it at the time, but I should have been suspicious when a new double bed was installed in the little bedroom that became mine when "the boys" (the term we always used for my brothers) were relocated in the basement. A *double* bed was purchased,

I soon realized, so that Grandma would have a place to sleep when she came to visit.

Looking back, I'm pretty sure that arrangement was no fun for Grandma, either, sharing a bed with a child. But come she did, and sleep she did, with me. In those days, I gave not a thought to her comfort—or lack thereof—so focused was I on my own misery. You see, Grandma was old (to me, she was always old, even when she wasn't very), and she *snored.* I don't mean your gentle, breathy snoring either. I mean the roof-raising kind. At least so it seemed to this youngster.

The trick was to get in bed and fall asleep before she did. Then I had a chance. But if I didn't happen to hit dreamland before Grandma entered snoreland, I was in trouble. Now Grandma, as you know, Mother, was a lovely, softspoken person who always wore an apron over her long-sleeved dresses. Except in church or at weddings and funerals, I never saw her in anything but a long-sleeved dress and apron. She was the living image of the old-fashioned grandma, right down to her sturdy old-lady shoes and her hair done up in a bun. And her hair was *long.* I don't mean medium long, I mean never having been cut in maybe forty years long. I didn't often get to see her take the pins out and redo the bun, but when I did I found the process fascinating. The bottom third of her hair was dark brown, and the top two-thirds was snow-white. Thus, she always had a dark bun set in the center of white hair.

Bittersweet

But I digress, which you are accustomed to by now, Mother. About the snoring. I remember complaining to you once, and you told me that sleepers generally snore only when lying on their backs, and that, without waking up, they will often take whispered suggestions to turn on their sides. You advised me to try it with Grandma the next time she kept me awake with her snoring. So, driven to desperate measures that very night, I whispered, "Turn over, Grandma." She sat straight up in bed and cried out, "Turn over where?" Embarrassed, and having no desire to explain myself, I didn't answer, but only mumbled a little as though in sleep. Grandma lay back down, on her side this time, and both of us went off to dreamland.

More memorable than her visits to our house were our visits to Grandma's farm house. I liked those better because there Grandma's bedroom was off-limits to children. I didn't have to share a bed with her. It really didn't strike me then, as a child, that you and your multitudinous siblings grew up together in that small house with none of the conveniences that we take for granted today. Not only was there just one "restroom," that one restroom was a little wooden structure down a rather lengthy path, and it served be the weather fair or foul.

I have very *un*fond memories of sitting in that little

wooden structure, cringing while the wasps buzzed in and out of their nest above my head. Worse still, the facility was not blessed with such luxuries as Charmin or Great Northern tissue. Pages (slick and stiff) from a full-colored Montgomery Ward or Sears and Roebuck catalogue (you remember that there was a Roebuck in those days) were provided, and not for reading, although reading was not forbidden unless someone was waiting outside. Which someone generally was. In fairness I have to say that each bedroom was graced with a "chamber pot" under the bed, placed there for the convenience of small children after dark and in winter.

Bathing at Grandma's was an adventure in itself, so long as we could go home at the end of our visit and climb into a porcelain bathtub, dated though it was, that had hot and cold running water at the turn of a tap. We never showered although there was a nozzle of some sort on the wall high above the tub. You, Mother, would not have the water wetting and staining your walls and window and floor, even after you installed plastic tiles around the tub. (It is not out of disrespect, but convenience, that today I shower freely and gladly. I'm sure you understand. You, however, remained a tub person until old age took away that option.) Actually, you had the luxury of two tubs as a child, both of them galvanized tin and portable. And I have been privileged to bathe in both of them, in birth order—the oldest in the family meriting the first bath, the youngest the last. In the same water, of course, which argues well for being the firstborn in a family.

One of the tubs was "store-bought," a round number three wash tub (from the wash house) of the same vintage as those depicted in Hollywood westerns. The bottom of that tub, however, was ribbed, which discouraged relaxation and also dawdling with rubber ducks and tiny handmade boats. The other tub, which was made by a neighbor who worked with tin, was long and narrow and much smoother on the bottom. There was one drawback, however. The bottom was not stiff and firm like that of the wash tub. Therefore, it gave with pressure and was wont to bloop up and down with even the slightest shifting of weight or position by the bather.

This singular feature produced not only interesting water and metal sound effects but also rather unique physical sensations in that part of the human anatomy used for sitting in tubs. Privacy was another concern in a house that had no bathroom. In winter, sheets were hung along one side of the round tub—the side opposite the coal stove where water was heated for one's bath and added as the tub cooled with successive bodies and the passage of time.

Summer was easier. The long tub was hauled out of the wash house and put in a sunny spot in the yard. Water was carried in buckets from the well and poured into the tub to be heated by the sun. Now that I think of it, Mother, I remember that it was easy enough to empty the tub in the yard when the bathing was finished, but how was the tub in the kitchen emptied? Maybe a siphon hose was used somehow. Since the house had no running water, it also had no drains. Why can't I recall that process? I suppose because we children didn't have to do it. Being required to take a bath outdoors in the portable tub was punishment enough.

In a sense, Mother, visiting your childhood home where Grandmother still lived was like revisiting your past, through my own eyes rather than yours: climbing the same apple and apricot trees that you climbed, wandering through the wild flowers on the hill above the house, playing in the granary, venturing deep into the root cellar among the parsnips and carrots, exploring the wash house, picking the wild plums that grew along the lane, watching Uncle Len milk the cows and taking an occasional squirt in the eye, spying on the boys swimming naked in the irrigation pond, going for water at the well by Aunt Jane's house, walking the long dusty road to Cudahy's (we always thought it was "Cuddy's") store for a Tootsie Roll or stick of licorice, calling on Aunt Jen in her home that once served as the school house you attended.

In my mind's eye, I can still see Grandma waving goodbye to us as we drive off in our old Plymouth. And as we

Bittersweet

leave, bumping slowly along, there you are beside us, Mother, a little girl tripping down the lane, calling back, guiltily and happily, "Goodbye, Mother! I'm going to school!"

Rhoda Clark (left) and friend. Rhoda (left with two friends. About 1924. Below: Rhoda (left) at age 17 with friend.

Page Six

Most of my memories of childhood with you are simple ones, Mother. Pages written large with few turns or twists. There is little in them of the drama and trauma that are the stuff of bestsellers. What there is in them is the stuff of life, ordinary life. What we had was stability. Priceless stability and constancy and love. Thus, I hit the road to adulthood on solid footing, knowing who I was and what was expected of me. As I said, it was predetermined that I would get good grades in school, that I would go to college, that I would know how to work. The truth is, following your example (and Dad's, for whom a twelve-hour work day and six-day work week were normal), my brothers and I became chronic workaholics. At least while we were salaried.

As I write this, I realize that even now I'm not happy unless I'm productive. I have to be writing or teaching or being useful in some capacity or other. Usually I'm going at all three and then some. (That's the *you* in me, Mother. You should see my calendar! One of these days I must learn to say "no" or to quit answering the telephone.) And so I concede that it is better to be a workaholic than an alcoholic or a drug-oholic or a play-oholic or any other kind of -oholic (except, of course, a choc-oholic). Maybe it is well after all that I spent much of my life trying to please you, trying to live up to your expectations. Otherwise, what might I have aspired to? What might I have done with my life? And I truly believe that the work has made the times of break from work, the times of restorative play, more delicious.

Winter is gone and it is now the end of May, the month of your death more than a decade ago, Mother; and as have I said, you are with me daily. But as I grow older in years I also grow in wisdom. The more I remember and the more I write, the less I blame you for anything, and the more happy times I recall. With the passing of years and the turning of pages, I realize all the more what kind of stamina and commitment it took for you to bring us through—and in the end, to bring Dad and yourself through. It seems to matter less, now, that we weren't "pals," much less "soul mates." I had enough friends. What I needed was a mother, and you were that with a capital "M." What you and I had, I see more clearly now,

Bittersweet

was good, oh so good, and perhaps it was enough.

You also had a special kind of sensitivity. Fussbudget though you were, Mother, you knew when to hold back, when not to add the hurt of criticism to an already hurting child. I don't believe I ever heard you say, "I told you so" when I ignored your counsel to my detriment. You seemed to know that reaping the consequences of my actions was reprimand enough. I remember one incident in particular. I was in the ninth grade, running for vice president or secretary (I don't remember which, which tells me how important such matters are in the larger scheme of things) of the student body at Washington Junior High School.

There was to be a big assembly where the finalists would be introduced and speak. Somehow you found the money to buy me a new skirt (store-bought, not home-made or hand-me-down!) for the occasion. It was a very light beige, almost cream-colored, skirt, and I thought it was beautiful. A couple of friends and I were planning to paint posters after school, and you cautioned me that morning to come home and change into jeans before working with paint. Well, I thought I knew better and couldn't be bothered to go home and change. I would be careful. Yes, the inevitable occurred. I spilled a big glob of bright green paint (and I do mean *bright*) down the front of my lovely new skirt.

Ashamed, heartsick about the skirt, and unwilling to face the music with you just then, I slipped into the house after the painting episode and hung the skirt in the very back of the small closet I shared with you. (Dad's clothing pretty much filled the equally small closet off your bedroom. Even with the few clothes we owned in those days, closet space was at a premium in our house.) The skirt was definitely a Sunday skirt, not a weekday skirt (girls did not wear pants to school in those days), and I put it out of my mind during the hectic days of the campaign. We made posters and flyers and participated in all the hoopla that went with school elections back then. Election day came and I lost. Crestfallen (worse still, defeated by an *eighth* grader!), I went home where you provided crackers, milk, and sympathy.

A few days later, my wounds now licked, I suddenly remembered the skirt and knew it was time to face the music. I went to the closet and found the skirt where I had "hidden" it. To my astonishment, the skirt bore no bright green stain. Instead, it bore a dry cleaning tag. You, Mother, had seen the stained skirt, but had said nothing to me about it. No recriminations, no scolding. You simply sent it to the cleaners and returned it sparkling to the closet. You, the ultimate fussbudget and penny wise parent! No, you the ultimate mother, who knew when not to add a burden of reproach to an already disappointed daughter. I went to you, skirt in hand, and wept tears of gratitude. You understood. For that moment, at least, we were no more strangers, but friends.

Bittersweet

Unlike many neglected and troubled children today, my brothers and I were constructed on a rock solid foundation. As the memories of my childhood rise irrepressibly to the surface, I am overwhelmed with tenderness. The ending of this book will not be the same as the beginning because the very act of writing it is changing me. I only wish you were here so that I could tell you. One day, one day, I will tell you in person. But now, move on with me to still more childhood memories. I find myself quite astonished that you are at the center of them all. You, Mother, were clearly the ever-present being, the principal reality, in my life. As I look back, how large you loom. Now that I think of it, you and I were together a lot. Maybe it was because you didn't drive, or because you didn't chum much with friends. Maybe it was because we always worked together, from the time I was big enough to wield a dish towel or dust cloth, or to place knife, fork, and spoon beside plates on the table.

It was good, I see now, working with you. There was the inescapable rite of Saturday cleaning, which ranked nearly as high on my scale of childhood delights as visits to the dentist, those sanctioned rituals of torture in vogue before the advent of novocaine and high speed drills. Or at least before anyone thought such pantywaist innovations necessary. In the matter of tooth decay, as in all matters in your house, there was no deviating from regular maintenance and repair. We went to the dentist once a year, and we cleaned house every Saturday.

Marilyn Arnold

The work to be done remained constant, but the various tasks rotated so children had no grounds for complaint of favoritism. Dusting furniture and wooden floor borders and baseboards fell to us, while you handled bathroom, kitchen, and (until I got old enough to do it "right") linoleum floor-waxing and vacuuming. In summer, of course, lawn-mowing (with a push mower) was added for any child with sufficient muscle power, and lawn sprinkling for any child with hands.

Because you taught school, Saturday was also wash day. We had an old wringer washing machine and a separate rinse tub, so clothes went through the ringer twice, and then were carted in a chipped white porcelain tub to the backyard and hung on lines winter (I can still feel their stiff crustiness) and summer. When a cousin lost two fingers in his mother's wringer, I was relieved of wringer responsibilities until I reached a riper age. I still remember the mysterious bottle of what you called "bluing," some of which you added to loads of white things in the washing machine. (Or was it the rinse water?) Having seen what a little blue coloring could do to a birthday cake, I was surprised that you risked it in the laundry. You told me that "bluing" was for whitening and warned me against experimenting with it in your absence. It was all I could do to leave that bottle alone. I think I tried some of it on snow once, with unsatisfactory results.

For many years, bed sheets and Dad's shirts went to the laundry where he worked, a perk that came with the job. Our one luxury. Once we children began working outside the home, after school and on Saturdays, and Dad changed jobs (to a five- instead of six-day work week when the Troy Laundry burned down), he took over the home laundering in the basement while you cleaned upstairs. That's right. Our undomestic father didn't cook or clean house, but he did laundry. Which amazed me. Because he knew how better than the rest of us, he said, and he was right.

In addition to Saturday chores, there were the daily things, like setting the table for supper and cleaning up after. From the time I was very young, certain tasks associated with supper were always assigned to me—things like cleaning celery and filling it with cheese spread packaged in small glasses with tin lids that when empty became our orange juice glasses. Other things like scraping carrots, peeling potatoes, and washing and topping radishes always fell to me. How I loved to come home from school and snack on radishes, which I dipped in salt and washed down with milk. (Milk took the sting out but left the taste.) Sometimes I did dishes with one of my brothers, but we tended to dilly-dally over the chore, unless it was summer and still light outside. You never interfered as we stirred up great mounds of soap suds by beating air into the dishwater with a glass or bottle. (You chose your battles, Mother, as they say.)

Marilyn Arnold

Most of the time, however, you and I did dishes together, you washing and I drying. If a glass or plate slipped out of my child's hand and shattered on the floor (this was before the days of sturdy childproof dinnerware), you never scolded. A scolding would have broken the spell of harmony that encased our labors like a magic bubble. In your wisdom you never risked it. Those dish washing and drying times were times not only for gabbing about nothing and everything of little consequence but also for singing together. We sang Primary songs and school songs and sad songs and happy songs. We sang songs your mother had sung to you, and songs it seemed no one else in the world knew but the two of us. We even sang "Catch the Sunshine," which tune was indelibly printed in our minds because of your piano renditions. We sang "Shine On," and "Jesus Wants Me for a Sunbeam," and "Oh, I Had Such a Pretty Dream, Mama." Neither of us was endowed with what you'd call a "public" singing voice, Mother, but we managed to carry a tune that served for private kitchen sink performances.

Your memories of those lovely times of "sink communion" in the old house were so precious to you that when you and Dad moved to Orem, after retirement, you chose not to install an electric dishwasher in your modest new quarters. You never felt the need to justify your decision to others, but I knew your reasons. People come together in nice ways over a kitchen sink, and you didn't want to lose that meeting, even

Bittersweet

if it was only you and Dad at the sink. To my amazement, he took over the drying duties when no one else was around. You finally domesticated him, sort of. (Maybe doing laundry broke him in!) In all the years I knew him, Dad never cooked a meal. His one contribution to food preparation was grinding wheat for morning mush (a winter routine) and taking you to the grocery store. I recall, too, that he had no trouble finding ice cream in the freezer section of the refrigerator. Vanilla. He never ventured past vanilla, while you and I were hooked on burnt almond fudge.

You and I had other "sink connections," too, Mother. One was the hair washing ritual. When I was small, every Saturday found me stretched on my back across the kitchen counter top, my head over the sink, while you shampooed my hair with lather from a bar of Ivory soap. (It was years before I graduated to the luxury of "real" shampoo.) Another important sink ritual was the canning of fruit in late summer. Actually, what we did was *bottling*, but in the local parlance it was "canning," and we were conformists in such things. As a child, I wondered why you called that big, blue pan with the wire frame inside a "cold pack canner," but I never asked. I just took your word for it, as I did for most things. Still, it seemed to me that "cold" was the wrong word for the process because the pan bubbled frantically on the stove

Marilyn Arnold

with its five bottles of fruit inside. I thought it nothing short of miraculous that those glass bottles didn't break in that boiling water.

My job was not to wonder about the cooking process. My job was to peel whatever it was you were stuffing (yes, stuffing raw, thus "cold," I later realized) into those Kerr Mason Jars, unless it was plums or cherries, which had only to be stemmed and washed. Peaches, pears, and apricots had to be halved and cored or pitted as well as washed and peeled. (Why on earth did we peel apricots, Mother? I suppose because Dad preferred them that way.) Apples had to be washed, halved, cored, peeled, and ground for apple sauce. Raspberries had only to be washed; tomatoes had to be washed and quartered. Oh yes, I knew the routine all right.

Anyway, Mother, I remember how wrinkly my hands got, reaching into a sink full of water where the fruit of the day was taking its bath. It's a wonder the thumb on my right hand has any print left, so many times did the paring knife blade meet it. (I just examined that thumb, for the record, and it appears to me to be smoother than its counterpart on my left hand. You could claim that years of gripping a tennis racquet or ski pole or hiking stick, not peeling fruit, had smoothed that thumb, but I would dispute it.) You also preserved grape juice and all kinds of jams and jellies. My favorite of your bottled treasures was a sweet sliced pickle you called "crystal cukes." Those thin flat circles were bright

Bittersweet

green and deliciously crunchy. They tasted like no other pickle on earth, and I remember rationing the slices of the last jar you ever canned to make them last. You also preserved a mustard pickle, which you and Dad liked, but which your children thought rather a waste of a good cucumber.

To tell the truth, Mother, I didn't mind the peeling and slicing there at the sink beside you. There were rewards in addition to your company because as we worked, I popped a good many of the skins with their sweet linings into my mouth. Maybe that's where I developed my extraordinary love of fruit. Even today, fruit is my favorite food. Next to home-made brown bread and chocolate. No, maybe fruit even outranks chocolate. Few things were more satisfying in those days than seeing the literal "fruits of our labors" lined up on counter tops before making their journey to the fruit closet in the basement. The fruits were beautiful in their shiny bottles, organized by kind and color—red, gold, white, purple, green. Sometimes I would go to the fruit closet just to admire them, row on row, lusciously filling the shelves, shelves that over the winter gradually gave up their enticing treasures in exchange for empty bottles. My consolation was that the cycling seasons would fill those jars again.

Now that I think about it, I wonder if you and I did anything in the summer but work. Somehow, though, I always wound up with a suntan that wouldn't wash off like other dirt, so I guess you weren't a heartless taskmaster. You finally convinced me that my tan was waterproof. We started summer vacation off on the "right foot," in your view, with spring cleaning. Fruit didn't begin ripening until late June, which gave plenty of time for spring cleaning. It was an annual event that made the end of school less attractive. (You taught fourth grade at Washington School where my brothers and I attended grades one through ten. There was no school lunch, so we walked the two and a half blocks home for lunch together. We were never far from the restraining influence of your motherly gaze and discipline, it seems.) As I was saying before roaming off the subject, the end of school meant not immediate freedom, as it should have to my child mind, but immediate spring housecleaning.

I confess, Mother, that I have not carried on the tradition. It is a rare spring (or summer or fall or winter, for that matter) that finds me doing a back to basics, thorough cleaning of every inch of my house. In fact, that kind of dreary event occurs mainly when I change residences and it is forced upon me. Which I seem to do with some regularity, probably as much to de-clutter my quarters as to start fresh in a different location. This doesn't mean that I live in squalor. My place is fairly tidy, so long as one doesn't inspect closets or garage, or object to stacks of papers on desk and counter-tops in den and library. Why do I feel the need to

Bittersweet

justify my ways to you even now, Mother? This current guilt trip is most surely brought on by memories of you and me in the middle of spring (in our case, *summer*) housecleaning.

As I mentioned earlier, our home was heated by a coal furnace and our walls were covered with patterned paper. That's how walls were done in the days before drywall supplanted sometimes rough plaster. A coal furnace meant dirty walls and woodwork. Dirty walls meant the wonder of wallpaper cleaner, which you purchased in soft pink bricks and molded into spongy balls. Annually, we worked those hand-sized globs across every wall and ceiling in the house, one stroke at a time, gradually reducing that bright pink glob to a smaller ball of streaky gray. I was always amazed at the light stripe that appeared with each swipe of the cleaner. The closer we were to furnace outlets, the more pronounced the contrast. That part was satisfying. What was not satisfying was being required to expend what you called "elbow grease" on undirty walls or ceiling in a closed bedroom that received heat only in brief periods when a child was sick in bed. You had your standards, and spring cleaning allowed no exceptions.

Of course, scrubbing and waxing the linoleum floors was no novelty. We did that every Saturday anyway, rain or shine, on hands and knees. These days my low-maintenance tile floors are lucky to get scrubbed once a month (seldom on hands and knees), and I have not cleaned a whole wall since I officially left your home to become a homemaker (of sorts) myself. Touch up cleaning has served me well over the years, and I do extra dusting only when expecting company. It isn't that you didn't train me thoroughly, Mother. Perhaps you trained me too thoroughly and my psyche rebelled.

I now find that I postpone housework until guilt (or impending company) drives me to it. As I think about it, perhaps what I really dislike is doing housework alone. I didn't necessarily like the work in those days, but I certainly didn't hate it when you and I did it together, when it was "our" project, when we were a team, singing or gabbing as we worked. In fact, there was one aspect of spring cleaning that I actually liked. You must have realized early on that I would be a book and word person. The bookcases in the living room were always assigned to me, and I was given a full day with them if I wanted it. I always wanted it.

Behind the two sets of glass doors that flanked the fireplace (originally dull red brick, later shiny ceramic tile) was a magical world of books. I was to remove each book and dust it, then stack it beside me until it was joined by all the books from one shelf. Then I was to clean that shelf thoroughly and replace the books, one at a time, keeping each in its proper order. How I treasured those books, most of which have disappeared somewhere, perhaps when you moved. One big red book (at least it seemed big to me then) was called *Illustrious Americans,* a who's who of American history. I remember that the spine was torn and frayed.

Bittersweet

Dad, who was an avid reader, must have spent a good many hours with that book. History and religious books were his choice, and sentimental poetry. (Surprise.) He had no use for fiction, though you did, Mother. And I did, and do. Curiously, there was a multi-volume set of books called *Popular Science* sharing space with Mother Goose and Elbert Hubbard. The books I dawdled over longest were your high school yearbooks, Mother. It was like rediscovering a stranger every time I opened them. Who was this bright-eyed girl in old-fashioned dress and dark, wavy hair? How was she transformed into a mother? And not just any mother, but *my* mother?

In those days, Mother, at least in our household, bed springs were not enclosed. They were open and exposed to dust. Therefore, they had to be cleaned annually, no dodging the task. In your rubric, cleaning did not mean wiping off in place. Cleaning meant hauling the wire monsters down the narrow back porch stairs, or up the narrow basement stairs, and leaning them one by one against the side of the garage. Cleaning meant squirting with the hose and then wiping each and every wire spring, around and around and down each ever-narrowing spiral. I liked the squirting part; I did not like the hauling and the wiping parts. When I was very small we must have had help with the hauling. I never had help with the wiping, however. We also had to remove all the window screens for squirting and cleaning. Nothing escaped you, Mother. No speck of dirt, no spider's web. And least of all your daughter.

I remember little things, too, Mother, like the twenty-dollar bill that would appear mysteriously from your cedar chest if an urgent, unforeseen need arose outside the weekly necessities and budget. Maybe I had to have a costume for a school program, or a new music book for my piano lesson. Maybe one of the boys needed something for a scout trip. Or maybe one of us had to go to the doctor to be stitched up after a fall. Whatever the need—and it seemed never to be your need—there was the magical reserve bill that saw us through until payday. Thrift, indeed, was your middle name.

I also remember the day Dad came home with an engagement ring for you. (Was it the same day he made the last house payment and tore up the mortgage? I didn't understand fully what a mortgage meant. Hadn't we always owned "our" house? But I knew it was cause for celebration.) It was a *real* diamond ring. No matter that the stone was so small we could hardly see it, we children were awestruck and you were dumfounded. You had a diamond ring at last. We teased you and Dad for getting things backwards, for marrying first and becoming engaged after. You treasured that ring, Mother, and kept it for best-dress occasions like church services. I wonder how long Dad saved for that ring, which probably cost less than two hundred dollars, much less. It might have been years.

Dad liked surprises, and he especially liked to surprise you after a long period of planning and saving. The surprise I remember best came at Christmas one year. I must have been eight or nine. About two weeks before Christmas, Dad arrived with a huge box done up in brown laundry wrapping paper. He wrote "For Mother" on it and set it by the Christmas tree (it was too large to go under the tree). Well, we were all curious; but you, Mother, could scarcely contain yourself. You were known as a "mover and a shaker" when it came to Christmas gifts, and we always took great delight in watching you shake packages and make wild guesses about their contents. You were great fun at Christmastime (and other times, too, I now realize). Dad sometimes let me in on his gift for you, even sent me shopping for it in later years, but not this year. None of us could imagine what that huge brown box contained.

Christmas morning came at last, but it was your gift we ran to first, Mother. Our own gifts could wait. We begged you to open the brown box first. You pretended patience, but we knew you were on pins and needles. I think you feared, however, that Dad had been too extravagant with the family's limited funds. Well, the moment arrived, and you tore off the wrapper, and inside was . . . another brown wrapped box. And inside that another brown wrapped box. And inside that another. And so on down through countless smaller and smaller brown wrapped boxes until you arrived at a very small, flat package. Inside it was a bank pass book that bore the record of savings (mainly) and withdrawals (a few) for the past ten years. (This was before computers, kids.) The balance was close to two thousand dollars, a huge sum for a laundry man to save up in those days.

You were flabbergasted, and didn't know quite what it meant at first. Then Dad explained. In all the years you and he had been married, he said, you had never called him to account for what remained of his paycheck after he gave you household money and paid bills. (We were a one-salary outfit in those days because you didn't return to full-time teaching until all your children were in school.) You had never asked if there was money left over, and if so, what he had done with it. Out of gratitude for your unwavering trust in him, he had saved whatever small amount was left after he met auto expenses and costs for home maintenance. And now he was giving it to you. Yes, you wept then, Mother. We all wept. Except Dad. He took you in his arms and smiled and smiled.

Bittersweet

Rhoda Clark Arnold, wife, mother and college graduate.
All the family attended the ceremony.

Marilyn Arnold

Rhoda Clark Arnold as a very much appreciated wife, mother, and teacher.

Page Seven

Maybe this is a good time to say more about Christmas, to revisit that blessed page of our lives. We had Christmas. Oh yes, we had Christmas. My favorite holiday as a child, by far. When I was old enough, you let me choose my Christmas gifts for others, parceling out the pennies, nickels, and dimes I had been secreting away for many weeks. How I loved to make things, too, and shop for things, and wrap things (always with white tissue paper, because it was inexpensive, and could be dressed up with colored stickers). I also loved to decorate the sweet-smelling tree you and Dad would bring home some December evening. Our main decorative extravagance each year was a new box of shiny foil icicles (which could end up strung entirely on one low limb if your lastborn toddler son was not restrained).

    I watched eagerly as you went to the hall closet and lifted tree decorations from the highest shelf where they had sat for eleven long months. I knew the shiny bulbs and strings of lights like old friends because I was required to dust each one, oh so carefully, before it could be hung on the tree. Over the years, we acquired additional ornaments and lights; but the red pendant with gold trim, the one you and Dad bought together for your first Christmas, was always installed in the place of honor, as I said, even when we added a lighted star to the mix later on.

Traditions. Formalities. Christmas was a beautiful time of tradition for us, Mother, and I remember feeling such a great rush of love and excitement that I could scarcely contain it. I lived whatever it was that people called "the Christmas spirit" to the nth degree. I simply fell in love with the season, with its music, its tinkling splendor, its surge of religious blessedness, its joyous anticipation. Jesus became more real for me when I thought of him coming into the world as a baby. I was filled with the joy of giving and receiving and celebrating. I'm not sure when all that changed, but change it did. The magic disappeared with the passing years.

You and I never talked about that, Mother. We just kept playing the game of holiday happiness well into my adulthood. It has been years now since I have put up a Christmas tree. You, however, reluctant to let tradition go when hauling and setting up a real tree became impossible, bought an artificial tree and decorated it faithfully every year. And when you and Dad could no longer assemble and decorate that tree, your firstborn son did it for you. Maybe Christmas

Bittersweet

lost its splendor for me because childhood vanished and took with it some of the cherished traditions honored in that small house with the coal furnace where peace dwelt in abundance.

Maybe if I had borne children of my own, I could have recaptured that humble splendor. But maybe, Mother, since I broached the subject above, I can rekindle the warmth of those years, for a moment anyway, by returning in memory with you to Christmases in that faraway time called childhood. Despite the emptiness that on Christmas Eve today can brink on despair, I do have to tell you that the worshipful music of the season still moves me, rescues me, as do the words of Luke and John, along with Nephi, Jacob, Alma, and prophets of this dispensation. And I like the warmth and generosity, the human kindnesses, that emerge with the season. What I long to hear now, however, is your voice gently asking:

> I wonder who is Santa Claus
> and from what land he comes,
> and where he got such pretty toys
> and nice sugar plums.
>
> In his cold home in ice-bound land,
> he travels swift as light.
> He travels all around the world
> in just one single night.

Marilyn Arnold

He wears a coat and cap of fur,
at least that's what they say.
And he has merry twinkling eyes,
and beard so long and gray.

Santa Claus was living
when Grandmother was young like me.
If he should die,
what would we children do?

In my mind, even as I write this, I hear your voice reciting Christmas poems—in low, mellow, softly modulating tones. Another Santa poem comes to mind:

Santa Claus, I hang for you
by the chimney, stockings two—
one for me and one to go
to another boy I know.

There's a chimney in this town
that you have never traveled down.
Should you chance to enter there
you would find that room quite bare.

Bittersweet

> Not a stocking you would find,
> matters how hard you might try.
> And the toys you'd find are such
> that no boy would care for much.
>
> In a broken bed you'd see
> someone just about like me,
> dreaming of the pretty toys
> that you bring to other boys.
>
> And to him a Christmas seems
> merry only in his dreams.
>
> All I wish for Santa Claus,
> fill my stocking. And when
> it's filled up to the brim,
> I'll be Santa Claus to him.

As I said earlier, Mother, no one knows the origin of your poems, Christmas poems included. Perhaps your mother plucked them from her mother's mind and fed your imagination with them just as you fed mine.

You were always at the center of our Christmas traditions in the small house in an old neighborhood, Mother (and you

Marilyn Arnold

carried the dessert traditions to Orem with you). First, there was the date pudding (I seem to remember it wrapped in cloth) topped with your special caramel sauce, the secret recipe handed down, like your poems and stories, from Grandmother. There was also fruit cake—dark brown and moist in my early years, almost white and full of nuts and high color (thanks to bright candied maraschino cherries and pineapple) in later years. You became more adventuresome as the years passed, investing endless time and energy in things we children simply took for granted.

Fruit cakes and date pudding were prepared in advance, as were the Christmas sugar cookies, made from your mother's recipe. You had cookie cutters in the shapes of Santas, trees, stars, stockings, and bells. (How readily we blended the Christian and the pagan!) When I became old enough to wield a variety of colored frostings without plastering half the kitchen with them, I was enlisted to decorate the cookies to take to neighbors. The stars and bells were pretty simple, but I remember getting creative with the Santas, stockings, and trees. They became multi-colored, as did I, in the process.

Once the frosting dried, we prepared plates of cookies which Dad then faithfully delivered to neighbors. The cookies were thick and creamy white, baked to perfection. Any that were deemed too thin for worthy gifts, or tinged with brown edges, were kept for our household. My wages consisted of licking the frosting bowls and eating some of the

Bittersweet

rejects. I have never tasted, before or since, sugar cookies that could measure up to yours, Mother. You used that same recipe to make filled cookies, which consisted of two flat cookies pressed together with a raisin mix in the center. Out of this world delicious. Maybe I had a special appreciation for the cookies and pies you baked because sugary treats were not daily fare in our house.

Even as my brothers and I grew older, we always spent Christmas Eve at home with you and Dad. No dates, no parties with friends, no leaving the house except together. We never made it a household rule; we never even talked about it. That we would be home, that we would be together, was simply understood. There was always the waffle supper, with scrambled eggs and bacon. There was the hanging of the stockings above the fireplace and (when we were very small) the note to Santa with a few cookies. There was sitting around the lighted tree and guessing what was in packages that bore our names, and you, Mother, as I said, shaking and shaking yours, making a game of guessing what they contained. (Of course, you purposely never guessed correctly. That would have spoiled everything.) There was singing of Christmas carols and then, finally, reading of the Christmas story from the second chapter of Luke in the King James Bible. I can still hear your voice, reading reverently: "And there were in the same country, shepherds abiding in the fields, keeping watch over their flocks by night." I could probably recite most of it, so deeply is it engraved in my memory.

And after that, it was off to bed, where I invariably spent a restless and wakeful night, so exhilarating was the anticipation of the morning. We children went to bed armed with flashlights, clocks with alarms set, and various instruments for making noise—pans to bang, spoons to bang them with, whistles, bugle, voices. We were not to make a peep before 6 a.m., though we knew friends who were allowed to get up at 4, open gifts, and then return to bed. At 6 a.m. sharp, we would begin the clatter.

Our first words were a shout: "Merry Christmas! Turn up the stoker!" We were not allowed to leave our warm beds in our cold rooms until the furnace had done its work in other parts of the house. At a sign from Dad, we converged at the door between kitchen and living room, a door that was almost never closed except on Christmas morning. We knew Santa would have come, but we were to enter the room together. No sneak previews were permitted in your house, Mother.

Then Dad would open the door and we would race to the tree. My gifts from Santa—a book (always), a new teddy bear, perhaps a new pair of pajamas, and one nice toy or game—would be in Dad's reading chair. The boys' gifts would be by the fireplace and the sofa. Then we would open our gifts from each other and watch you and Dad open your

Bittersweet

gifts. One at a time. There was no random tearing into wrapping paper and boxes. Oh no. Gifts were opened one at a time, slowly, while the rest of the family watched with great respect and interest. No one opened out of turn. Money was not plentiful, but our expectations rarely exceeded the gifts. We were trained to keep expectations modest.

One large gift was granted each child on her or his ninth Christmas. A bicycle. My brothers received new bicycles (one was pre-war, the other post-war). On my ninth Christmas the country was still under the effects of war shortages, and there were no new bicycles to be had, just as there were no new automobiles. Thus, my secondhand wheels from the "Missouri Waltz" woman next door. There were not even sleds with steel runners. (My younger brother received a home-made sled with wooden runners.) As I noted earlier, virtually all steel and rubber produced in those years went into the war effort, leaving little for domestic consumption. (Can anyone born after 1945 even conceive of such a world?)

I loved Christmas so much as a child, Mother, that I could not bear for the glorious day to be over, the day I had waited for so long. As Christmas day faded into evening, Dad would invariably, unknowingly, break my child's heart by launching into the saddest song in the English language.

Marilyn Arnold

(Even sadder, Mother, at least for me, than your mournful song of the lost babes in the woods. Not only do I remember your singing of the babes to me, but I remember your singing of them to your first and only granddaughter when she was a pre-schooler. I can still see her crying big tears as you sang it, and begging you to "sing it again, Grandma, sing it again," while she sobbed away.) Oh, how I dreaded the song that confirmed Christmas was over. I silently begged Dad not to sing it. I wanted to close my ears and run, but it was always too late; I always heard it:

> Dinner is done, night has come,
> worn and tired are they.
> Gun won't shoot, horn won't toot,
> blocks all lost but ten.
> But never fear, just wait one year,
> old Kris will come again,
> fill well the stockings
> and leave without a sound.
> No girl or boy is filled with joy
> 'til good ol' Kris comes 'round.

I never told Dad that his little song made me unbearably sad. Did I tell you, Mother? Soon enough, I grew up. Soon enough, I was glad when Christmas night came.

H. Lynn Arnold worked in the laundry business for many years. Later he made good use of the experience by sharing family chores.

Marilyn Arnold

Dad, H. Lynn Arnold.

Page Eight

Memories of your traditional Christmas cooking and baking open yet another page, Mother, one that reminds me of your willingness to take the trouble to do special things in special ways. You just plain took the trouble while I just plain don't. Over the years it became obvious to both of us that the last thing I would attempt is Christmas pudding or cookies of any kind from scratch. (Extemporaneous soup, I can handle, however. It's called clean out the refrigerator.) I think all of us (except you, perhaps) more or less took your cooking skills for granted. For years you didn't get a chance to display much imagination in the kitchen because Dad was basically a meat and potatoes man.

He had good reason to be because his mother died when he was very young, and his father (who was a machinist at the Bingham Copper Mine) arranged for his children (of whom there were seven) to eat with the miners at the local boarding house. Miners, as a rule, do not favor crepes and

Marilyn Arnold

egg plant over roast beef, mashed potatoes, and gravy. And neither did your own father and brothers and brothers-in-law, most of the them being farmers. You indulged Dad's simple tastes, but you also branched out, gradually nudging him into new delights of the palate.

Some foods became your trademark in cuisine. I described several of your Christmas specialities earlier, but they are not the only splendid dishes in your recipe bank. First to my mind is "Aunt Rhoda's Baked Beans," so named by your niece (my cousin) who adopted the recipe. It even appears in print, from a major publishing house, under that heading. (I was asked to submit something for a collection, and having nothing of my own devising to contribute, I confiscated your recipe. It does bear your name, however.) You also made a scrumptious meat loaf, a variety of stews, and a delicious riced potato and cheese dish. Your white bread was crusty and hearty, your date bread moist and chewy, your perfect banana cream pie beyond description. (How I loved the leftover strips of pie crust, baked and sprinkled with cinnamon and sugar.)

Most memorable, perhaps, were a couple of desserts that I never encountered anywhere else. One, a lemon wonder of unknown ingredients (except lemons), and the other something you called "Chocolate Syrup Dessert." The title doesn't do it justice. It should have been called heavenly some-

Bittersweet

thing or other. My younger brother, your lastborn son, telephoned today to report that his wife had just made that lusciously wicked dessert for him, as a special nostalgic treat, for Father's Day. (He had the good fortune to fall in love with a woman who is a marvelous cook.) Knowing what was in that dessert didn't deter me from wolfing it down when, in my blissful innocence, I gave not a thought to such unpleasantries as cholesterol and heart disease. But now, well now, the days of innocence are over. Fat in the arteries is making the evening news; the days of antioxidant and cholesterol tyranny are upon us.

Every package of everything edible contains its guilt list printed on the container: calories, trans fat, saturated fat, sugar, sodium, and so on. How could I now eat your delectable desserts, or your date pudding (with its incredible caramel sauce), or your twice-baked potatoes (with their sour cream and cheese) knowing that their ingredients could trigger cardiac arrest or worse in an instant? Your chocolate dessert, for example, contains, at a very minimum, eggs, whipped cream, Hershey's canned chocolate syrup, walnuts, and miniature marshmallows. Bottomed with crumbled cookie crust and topped with whipped cream. Totally unhealthy and totally wonderful. In the matter of victuals, there's a lot to be said for ignorance.

Then there was your famous cranberry salad, with its fresh ground cranberries, celery, nuts, pineapple, and other chopped things, all set in lemon jello. (Granted, it was a while before Dad was converted to jello filled with so much stuff.) Oh yes, Mother, your dexterity with Jello was something to behold. The company should have put you on its payroll. And there was your "slush." That's all we ever called it, but it merited a more exciting name than that. I remember that its base was home-canned (i.e., bottled) grape juice, but there were other juices (citrus and pineapple?) in it. You froze it in ice cube trays (yes, kids, in the old days we froze ice cubes in trays because refrigerators weren't as smart as they are now) and served it in glasses on special occasions, with ginger ale to mush it up. It had to be ginger ale; no 7-Up or Sprite for you.

The list of your dinner delights could go on and on, but I'll spare you and try to stay out of the refrigerator (and the chocolate) for the next little while. (Ah, the power of suggestion. I just weakened and went for a bit of dark chocolate. I think it is good for the soul as well as the brain, don't you?) Truly, Mother, writing about these things has produced not only a craving for chocolate, but revelation upon revelation for me. It appears that I have taken your cooking skills for granted, as I have taken so many things about you for granted. I am in awe, and it is about time.

Why didn't I follow in your culinary footsteps, cooking up a storm or two? It is true that in my middle years I ventured to

Bittersweet

prepare a few dishes and meals that took a bit of doing. I was even known to have people over for supper occasionally. Now, I confess, I never do. You, Mother, if not appalled, would at least be disappointed. Your only daughter is getting lazier and lazier (or smarter and smarter!) about entertaining. For some reason (can I blame it on long legs?), standing at the kitchen counter and sink makes my back ache. And it seems to me that cooking is largely standing at the counter and sink, chopping or some such. An aching back goes with the territory.

It's the same with vacuuming and floor-mopping. Oh, the ache is dreadful. But I can climb up and down mountains with a pack strapped to my back for hours with scarcely a complaint. And play rowdy tennis singles for a couple of hours with nary a twinge. And stand lecturing to adoring crowds with not a single symptom of spinal discomfort. (If they are not adoring I can get symptoms.) What does that tell you? I have a very accommodating back, a back that is highly intelligent and selective in what it chooses to grumble about, and I intend to keep it happy.

As I write this, Mother, it is nearing 5 p.m., and I have given not a thought as to what I might eat for supper. I do a mental scan of the refrigerator and know that it contains much fresh fruit, naturally (forgive the pun)—apricots from a friend's tree, cantaloupe, blueberries, apples, oranges, strawberries, bananas (yes, Mother, contrary to your advice, and the advice of banana growers who want them to ripen and rot fast so we toss them out and buy more, I put bananas in the refrigerator), and such things as: leftover Brussels sprouts (microwaved), leftover baked beans (from a can), Swiss chard and carrots from a friend's garden (to be microwaved), tomatoes from another friend's garden, fresh broccoli (to be microwaved), fresh corn on the cob (to be microwaved) fresh sugar snap peas (to be eaten raw like candy), avocado, celery, carrot juice, and the usual romaine lettuce, onions, yam, and red potatoes. And this is not all by any means. I also have low-fat and non-fat dairy products. So you see, Mother, I make do with healthy fare and save my back for more important endeavors.

Most certainly, my domestic deficiencies (and they are legion) cannot be laid on you, Mother. You set the example. Why, you even embroidered and crocheted. (And I know women today who do such things, who take the trouble. They remind me of you, and I love them for it.) In fact, it might surprise you to know that I still display a framed embroidery piece you made for me once. It pictures three adorable owls on a limb, two of them upright and the third upside down. The embroidered heading reads "Nobody's Perfect." I chuckle and think of you every time I see it. Why did I used to assume that you expected perfection of me?

You got me started on embroidery once long ago, but

Bittersweet

soon enough I found reasons to abandon it. (Doesn't the Bible say that one should avoid even the appearance of evil? I interpreted that to mean don't let certain things like fancy stitch work get a toe in your life or conscience.) Besides, sewing was mainly an indoor activity, and I was mainly an outdoor child. And most sewing involved tiny needles that had to be threaded. Darning socks was about all I could handle as a youngster. That enterprise came under the category of the necessary rather than the optional. I didn't have a choice. Thankfully, darning needles had larger thread holes.

Darning socks is one of the things I did to earn my keep, along with ironing—easy flat things first, Dad's handkerchiefs, mainly. (I learned early that fathers were handkerchief people, children were Kleenex people, mothers were either or both.) Then I progressed to pajamas (yes, we ironed pajamas in your house, didn't we?) and finally shirts. Collar first, then sleeves, then inside front plackets, then one side front, then shoulder, then back, then other shoulder, then other side front. I still iron (when I get around to it) shirts and blouses that way. You taught me well, Mother, but you won't catch me at the ironing board very often these days. (I notice that my wrinkle-prone cotton things tend to remain in the closet while my wash-and-wears get washed and worn over and over again.)

Marilyn Arnold

Did it seem to you that almost nothing you labored to teach me (with the possible exception of ironing), by either precept or example, stuck? Again, are we a most unlikely mother-daughter pair? You might be surprised to know that almost daily now I send grateful thanks from knees to heaven that I was blessed to have been your child, blessed to have been reared by you and Dad. Blessed to have been nurtured in a home where children knew they were loved. I keep saying it, I know; but it is a growing insight for a woman no longer young, and it keeps coming out of my fingers, insisting. Whatever might have been missing from our relationship in my teen years and later, it is not nearly so important as the certainty, devotion, honor, sacrifice, and caring that were simply there, abiding without fanfare or even conscious recognition in our home.

That indefinable feeling of wholeness, of worth, that characterized our lives as children is what has made all the difference in my life as an adult. As a child I never felt anything but whole and worthwhile when I was around you. Even when you corrected me, or fussed (excessively, so I thought back then) over something, I never felt broken or unloved. Even when I grew older and couldn't confide in you, there was no weakening of the bond. That bond was established in childhood, and it held. Why else would some of my fondest memories be of Christmases past? Why else would I remember so many good things, like the fact that even when I was well

Bittersweet

established in a home of my own, I never left your house without something good to eat in my hands (and often in my tummy)? You continued to do special things for me, to mother me and feed me almost to the very end.

I remember one day, when I was on the brink of getting wisdom, I said to you that I felt a bit apologetic about not being like you, not doing the things you took the trouble to do, and to do well. (One of your sayings was, "If it's worth doing, it's worth doing well." I don't really agree with that now, especially because I dabble in a multitude of enjoyable things and perfect few, if any, but I see your point.) You, who had already arrived at wisdom, said consolingly, "You have other gifts, dear." And so I do, I suppose.

A friend once gave me a varnished piece of rough wood with wire attached for hanging. Obviously homemade, it bore a simple painting of sun, sky, and pines; and it bore the words, "Her gift, the gift of knowing each day that it is good." Maybe it's all right that I have never made a date pudding, or a pie, or filled a cookie—and never will. Or roasted a turkey, or made dressing, or mastered a hundred other things that were second nature to you. I was still yours, and you told me I had worth. How grateful I am for those simple words: "You have other gifts, dear," and for words long ago sewn by your hand on cloth, just for your only daughter: "Nobody's Perfect." Thank you, Mother. Thank you my dear, dear Mother.

All right, enough of this business about your domestic skills and my lack thereof. Let's move on, you and me, to other memories of our lives together in Ogden. I remember the day Dad came home with a mongrel dog in the car (or was it the laundry van?). He had rescued the dog out on a country road where he was making a delivery or picking up an order. The poor pooch had been abandoned and was half-starved. He was so scrawny that at first I thought he had no ears. I wasn't sure how you felt about acquiring a mutt, Mother, but you didn't object in front of your children. Having grown up on a farm, you were used to having dogs around, but you laid down strict ground rules. The dog would not be allowed in the house, and the children would be required to feed and care for it.

Dad went to work fashioning a dog house out of a wooden barrel that he painted and mounted on short two-by-fours behind the garage. High and dry even in winter. We called him "Pal," and with food, a good scrubbing, and tender care, he became a rather handsome fellow. His wavy hair was a mix of brown and black on his back and head, but white on his chest, feet, nose, and the tip of his tail. Before long his ears became visible, standing up smartly when he was on the

Bittersweet

alert for his canine enemy next door, the short-haired, ill-tempered Skippy. Pal was friendly with everyone and everything except Skippy and motorcycles.

As it turned out, the boys soon lost interest in Pal, but you and I never did, Mother. We worried over him if he didn't come home when we called, or if he got sick. We fed him and petted him and played with him on the grass in our backyard. Dad fixed a lengthy rope leash for him that would slide along one of the wire clothes lines stretched between poles across our backyard. The plan was for Pal to run happily back and forth along the line. He, however, didn't understand the plan. What he did was run in circles around shrubs and trees until his rope was so tangled he couldn't move. That kept him home, all right, except when we let him run loose for a while every day. Pal was a dear dog, true to his name.

I can see him now, when you or I detached his collar from the leash and granted him a period of freedom. He would dash down our driveway, lickety-split, circle the tree in the neighbors' front yard, and race back to us before taking off to explore the world. You always said that he came back to thank us for freeing him, and I believe you were right. Much as he loved his release, he usually came obediently when we went outside and called, "Here, Pal, here Pal." (Neither of us could whistle worth beans.) Then one day, a few short years later, he was hit by a car and killed. I don't remember burying our dear Pal. Dad must have taken care of that. He always seemed to

Marilyn Arnold

know what to do in any situation. You and I, Mother, cried together over Pal's death. The boys, it seemed to me then, scarcely noticed. He had not become part of their lives.

We may not have been wealthy as the world measures wealth, Mother, but we were rich in all the ways that counted. Fortunately for me, though as a child I didn't fully appreciate my good fortune, we were a church-going family. No ifs, ands, or buts. Early on, before you started back to school in earnest, you were a counselor in the Stake Primary presidency. I didn't know quite what that meant, except that it was at least moderately important. Maybe not as important as being Bishop of the Twenty-eighth Ward, which Dad was for several years, but important nonetheless.

I remember going to Primary after school (on Tuesdays, I think) until I was twelve (or almost), and then to evening gatherings of the Mutual Improvement Association (we just called it "Mutual" or "MIA"), the Church youth organization. Later, you taught in the MIA before serving (close to a life sentence!) as Junior Sunday School coordinator. Some of those years, while I was still in the nest, I played the piano—or played at it—for the Junior Sunday School. I'd be hard-pressed to do such now.

Yes, we were active members of the Church of Jesus Christ of Latter-day Saints, but everybody just called us

Bittersweet

"Mormons," after the name of the ancient prophet who abridged the record now called *The Book of Mormon*. We always walked to Sunday services together, three and a half blocks (I counted), because you didn't drive and Dad had early meetings. It took fifteen minutes if we clipped along. (You might not have been an Olympic runner, Mother, but oh, how you could walk!)

Your faith, Mother, was sure. So was Dad's. I never doubted that both of you believed the things I was taught in Primary and MIA and Sunday School. And as I have aged, I can see that the solidity of our home, its grounding in you and Dad, was anchored in your unwavering faith in the Gospel of Jesus Christ. The older I get, the more important these things are to me, too. You and I didn't talk much of your (or my) personal faith, but I always knew yours was there and trusted that one day I would know as you did. And now I do know, and know that I know.

A few more things come to mind about our life together in my childhood home in Ogden. Call them little odds and ends, snippets from well-worn pages. They make me smile. You always used to say that your firstborn son was spoiled because he was the first child, that I was spoiled because I was the only girl, and that your lastborn was spoiled because he was the youngest child. You were right, Mother, we were

Marilyn Arnold

all "spoiled" to some extent, I guess. But none of us "rotted." I am, however, as the years ruthlessly pile up, experiencing what one of my friends calls "the delicate ruin." I watched you grow old but never expected it to happen to me. I figured I could outrun old age. Ha!

Looking back, I remember that I was assigned (or volunteered, because you made fudge that was to die for—another of your specialties, along with divine divinity) to bring a batch of fudge to school (I was in high school then) for something or other. My plan was to get up and make it before school. You found your recipe the preceding night and handed it to me. It was called "Seven-minute Fudge." As I went merrily off to bed, I asked you to wake me seven minutes earlier than usual so that I could make the fudge. You laughed and wakened me *thirty* minutes earlier than usual.

You were always such a realist, Mother! And speaking of getting children out of bed in time for school, it was your firstborn highschooler, not your only daughter, who had to be dragged out of bed kicking and screaming every morning. It's a wonder he ever made it to school for his first class. When he did get up, he set land speed records getting his duds on and his morning mush swallowed.

In the matter of child spoilage, however, I have to say that my personal vote would go to your lastborn son, the original procrastinator (back then, not now by any means). That was when the only word processor known to

Bittersweet

humankind was the manual typewriter (of which I still have one, an Underwood, just in case at some point I am stranded on a desert island—or in my own garage—with no electricity). We had a black Royal typewriter, a machine which your now engineer, business executive, computer-savvy son never mastered. That meant you would type his class papers for him, and you were no whiz on the Royal either.

Still, this would not have been so bad if he had managed to finish writing his opuses (opi?) before 11 p.m. the night before they were due. He would sheepishly hand you the scribbled pages and descend to his bedroom. Since my bedroom was just off the kitchen, I could hear the clickety-click of the typewriter, in the kitchen, of course, going well into the wee morning hours. I seem to remember, too, that you washed and ironed his shirts, Mother, when he came home from college on a weekend. Shameless spoilage, but I have forgiven both of you. (I seem to remember that you had my fudge well underway when I arose that long ago morning, and that I was granted a store-bought formal for at least one prom.)

Marilyn, hiking Sulfur Creek in southern Utah's Capitol Reef.

Page Nine

Memories of every stripe keep charging into my mind, Mother, almost competing for attention. Thus, a narrative that I had thought would be somewhat chronological, at least after the introductory chapter, runs its own unpredictable course, plucking pages along the way as I race to catch up. Back and forth we go, up and down, around and around, with little apparent rhyme or reason. You could accuse me of random sampling, and you would be at least partially right. Nonetheless, I have known for years that anything I am writing takes on a life of its own. Much of the time I seem merely along for the ride. Take the present moment, for instance. My mind, rather unexpectedly, has filled with an odd assortment of things I never told you, never felt comfortable sharing. And still don't, I guess. It's as though you were actually present. I think it has always been simpler for me to operate on the assumption that there were things you preferred not to know. Did you, Mother, ever do underhanded things (aside from semi-innocent hard-boiled egg exchanges and child dehydration) that you weren't especially proud of? It doesn't seem possible. Or have I mentally cloaked you in a gown of perfection, unfairly allowing you few human flaws and foibles? In any case, how could I have bared my soul to you when I was certain (was I wrong?) that you would respond with either embarrassment or disapproval, or both? Again, maybe I dreaded your disappointment even more than your disapproval.

I find myself asking now, "Who are you, Mother?" Were my earlier images of you so partial and limited as to be completely unreliable? Is my current image of you, a picture growing ever more various, ever more precious and dear with the passing years, also partly fabrication? Is it the product of a little healing distance as well as deepening appreciation and measureless affection? Possibly, maybe even probably; but just the same, it is the image I want to keep. In the naivete of youth I made you two-dimensional. That was not truth either. I can see now that you had dimensions and depths of understanding I never fathomed.

A couple of summers ago I made my way to a cousins' reunion attended by your two surviving sisters and nearly all the living children of your multiple siblings. (Some cousins are gone already, your firstborn among them, a few long before their time.) Your lastborn son, still young-looking and vital, handed me three photo albums to leaf through—

albums you filled, albums I didn't know existed though many of the pictures are familiar. Why didn't you and I sit side by side and relive the past together in those albums, Mother? As I scan the cellophane-covered pages now, memories flood my mind and I see evidence that you were indeed many-dimensional.

There you are—a young girl in cotton dress, a young woman, a young wife and mother, and so on down the years until your hair turns silver and your eyes refuse to focus. There you are with friends, with family, at home on Christmas, at Grand Canyon on a rare vacation. There you are with babies in your arms, or a child sitting or standing beside you on the lawn or steps or driveway of our little house on Ogden Avenue. There you are with Dad, years ago and not so many years ago, too. There you are in cap and gown, your smiling face affirming that you did it! And yes, there you are in faded burgundy jump suit, scarf tied through your hair, just as I remember.

Yes, I am old enough (and you are safe enough) for a little honest confession. I assume that you are beyond mortal shock, that you now enjoy the largess of an eternal perspective. As I have said, in mortality you were anything but adventuresome when it came to activities in the outdoor world. This was my rationale for choosing not to burden you with tales of my outdoor escapades and sometimes narrow escapes. Other than tending garden and walking familiar streets, once you left the farm you became basically an indoor sort of person.

You, Mother, could not understand my passion for desert stream and sand, for red rock and sky, for mountain peaks and wilderness. You must have been perplexed at the fact that a daughter of your flesh was so different from yourself. It was obvious to me that if I were to describe my back country adventures in detail, you would magnify the dangers and discomforts and make yourself miserable with worry every time I went off with pack and hiking boots. Or skis and poles. At least so I reasoned.

I have to remind you, and myself, Mother, that for many years you taught fourth-graders, which took more stamina and daring than I could ever muster. Once when I was home on semester break from graduate school in Wisconsin, I taught—no, *tended*—your class so that you could travel to an out-of-town funeral. The experience was a revelation. This is what you did every day! And loved it! And never contemplated suicide (or homicide)! For me, that one day of subbing in an elementary school classroom confirmed the wisdom of my decision to teach college students rather than fourth-graders, or any other graders.

You hated to retire, to leave your beloved classroom (of fifth-graders, by then, at a new school). Me? I gladly took an early retirement—from pantyhose and pinching shoes and gainful employment—and entered the world of daylong comfortable clothing, bare feet, sloppy sandals, and *un*gainful employment. In other words, I became a writer, officially. I have always written a great deal, but for years I churned out mainly academic stuff and church stuff. In those days writing was a sideline, something I did nights, weekends, and holidays. Now it is a mainline. Now it defines me (when I can get at it between board meetings, committee meetings, church meetings, community functions, speaking engagements, yard work, tennis games, hikes, and so on.)

Ah yes, I see that I have strayed from my subject once more. It seems that true confessions are not my style. Excuses are more my style. You, Mother, are not surprised. Instead of rambling endlessly about things I never told you (some of which I alluded to earlier and some of which you may have suspected anyway), let me just mention a few more and then we'll get on with our life together as I remember it.

For instance, there was the time a friend and I skipped high school and went to Salt Lake City on a lark. I was hardly an habitual truant, but it was Spring and I felt a little wicked. The next day I forged your signature on an excuse for the principal's office. You found out, however, because my blabbermouth friend told her mother and she in turn told you. Some girls were not afraid of their mothers' displeasure. Some girls' mothers, I learned, were not overly disturbed by a daughter's rare frolic outside established boundaries. In my mind, you were not one of those mothers.

I wish I hadn't been afraid of your displeasure. Why was I? That question leads me to wonder about your relationship with your mother. You rarely spoke of it in personal terms, and I never asked. Of course, she had seven daughters to worry about while you had only one, which gave you a lot more time for worrying about that one. For the most part, I kept things from you (or "failed to mention" them) out of a desire to shield you from anxiety and sleep loss (and, I admit, to keep you off my case!). It was mainly outdoor exploits that put me at risk, and as I said, I didn't want you to fret every time your only daughter ventured into the wilderness.

By keeping mum and underplaying potential dangers (like bears in our camps in the high Sierras, which did happen, of course) and actual dangers (like wild river rapids that trapped me for what seemed aeons beneath a thrashing, bumping overturned rubber raft in eastern Utah; or a slip of the foot on a sheer wall that left me dangling a thousand feet above solid ground on the Grand Teton; or lightning storms that made my hair stand on end on Timpanogos Peak, and again on even craggier Lone Peak; or thunderstorms that wiped out a camp or two in the high Uintas; or downpours that could have triggered flash floods as I backpacked long, deep slot canyons in the remote desert; or blinding rain that drenched my bicycle and me, turning steep winding roads into slippery rivers as I raced down from Mirror Lake to Heber City in holiday camping and boating traffic). And these are just a few of the episodes that come to mind. I have chosen to spare you the more disquieting details.

Worrying is what you did best, and as I have said, you did many things well. Dad used to say it worried you if you didn't have anything to worry about, and he was probably right. I know now, if I didn't then, that your concerns for my safety, for the safety of all your children, and Dad, too, were driven by love. You couldn't bear for anything harmful to happen to any of us. Was it wrong of me to try to protect you by keeping you in the dark? Or was my motive less pure than that? I suspect it was a mix. I didn't want you to worry, but then again, I didn't want to *hear* you worry either. (I wouldn't call it nagging, what you did, Mother; that sounds too negative. Let's call it verbal "stewing.")

So there you have it. Self-interest always muddies the waters of my good intentions. I admit it, sometimes you had good reason to worry, whether you knew it or not. Although it's true that I escaped many things unscathed, I did sustain a fractured leg (broken in five places, you remember) in a skiing accident, and a subsequent severe bone infection. Those events could hardly be kept under wraps. You were living next door at the time. I remember how tenderly you cared for me through those difficult early weeks before the pain finally subsided (and I could begin playing tennis on a rolling chair and negotiating steep mountain trails with crutches and full leg plaster cast!). Maybe care-giving, not worrying, was what you did best after all.

Memories of that broken leg have taken me to the time when we shared a duplex in Orem. A dear friend and I occupied one side; you and Dad occupied the other. We shared many lovely things in those seven years. Some of my favorite memories of that time (and later times, too) are centered in the cherry harvest. Our grassy backyard was home to three large sweet cherry trees and one smaller sour (pie) cherry tree. Oh, how those trees produced! I was responsible for the harvest, though Dad helped pick in the early years. One spill off the ladder, however, sealed his fate. You forbade him to climb a ladder thereafter, though he still helped from the ground. I performed the ladder and limb acrobatics required to get the highest cherries while you and Dad sounded warnings from below.

When it came to preserving the precious fruit, we practiced division of labor. Dad had built a large drying box and outfitted it with several removable screen racks. He installed an electric fan to circulate warm air inside the box for quick drying. (Was there anything he couldn't build or repair?) We

Bittersweet

became a production line, out there in and under the trees. I picked, Dad pitted (one cherry at a time) with a nifty little device, and you washed and placed the cherries individually on the racks. Dad then put each full rack in the drying box. (Many is the evening on the trail that I poured boiling water from a blackened tin pot onto dried cherries, reconstituting them in my Sierra cup. They made a delicious dessert.) These memories are so insistent, Mother, that I am this very moment heading to the refrigerator where a few fresh cherries remain from someone else's tree and someone else's picking. They are not so good as our cherries were, but they will serve.

A few times, when we got a bargain on pineapple or some other fruit, we expanded our drying repertoire to include them. Years when we had a bumper crop, which was usually, it took at least two weeks to complete the sweet cherry harvest. We gave away pounds and lugs of cherries, to neighbors and relatives, and to the Bishop's Storehouse for the needy. We were not into selling cherries. The cherry harvest brought us close, Mother, the way Spring cleaning used to. We laughed and gabbed out there while above us the sun and birds did their thing. Once again, we were working together, and the artificial barriers that mothers and daughters sometimes construct fell away. How I wish I could recapture those days. Maybe in writing about them I have, for a moment anyway.

I find myself smiling. You seemed untiring then, and happy. That backyard was full of ripe cherries and ripe love.

Marilyn Arnold

We had other times of togetherness, too. The memories are flooding back now, the pages flying. Lovely they were. Well, maybe not always *perfectly* lovely. When your grandsons were yet small, and your lastborn son lived in the Salt Lake City area, I sometimes took his boys (there were no girls) on a special summer outing. One particular summer the plan was to go into the mountains above Heber City where we could hike and then sleep in the cabin of friends. The youngest son of your firstborn and the three oldest sons of your lastborn made up my hiking crew, and you, Mother, came along to give me a hand. Sleeping in rustic cabins was not your idea of a good time; but you volunteered, and so off we went, boys in the back of my 4-WD rag-top Scout, you and I in the front. The boys ranged in age from four or five to nine. All had their day packs, which packs almost dwarfed the two smallest adventurers. You, naturally, elected not to join us on the trail. Although you were an avid walker, paved walkways were your trails of choice.

As it turned out, you made a good decision. After we had walked a couple of miles, clouds gathered and rain came pouring down. What had been a dry dirt trail in the woods quickly became thick, gooey mud. It stuck to our boot soles and sucked at our feet with every step. There was nothing to do but abandon the hike. So I put the oldest boy in charge, found a semblance of shelter for the soggy trekkers under spreading pine bows, then took off to get the Scout and drive

Bittersweet

as near to the trail as the now muddy road would allow. On my return, the oldest boy and I loaded the younger ones—muddy messes we all were—on board and headed back to the cabin where you awaited us.

Leaving the boys' boots in the Scout, I carried each soggy youngster to the door. You lifted the little ones inside and took their wet, muddy packs and clothes off, cleaned them up, and got them into their pajamas. You also had cocoa and hot soup ready for the bedraggled crew. One thing you were, Mother, was able. You did what needed to be done with dispatch and good will. Not a single complaint did you utter, though you must have been miserable. Instead of ruing your own lot, you gave comfort to your grandsons.

You knew you wouldn't sleep a wink up there, and you didn't. But you were willing to go anyway. Unfortunately, wet boys and mud were not your only trial that day. You were prone to nosebleeds, and the high altitude triggered a nasty one that evening. Again, you were a good sport through an ordeal that lasted the better part of an hour and frightened us both. I don't give you enough credit, Mother. It's only in remembering things like this that I realize you were no sissy. Whatever came up, you could handle it. Why then do I typically think of you as fragile? Why is my lasting conception of you a delicate one? Is it because some part of you aspired to be a "lady' in the eyes of the world, and even in your own eyes?

I remember how pleased you were one day when you received a card of appreciation from a friend. She wrote that you represented to her what a true "lady" was. Being of a younger, supposedly more enlightened, generation, I pridefully thought that, in reality, you were paid no compliment. I personally wanted to regard myself as a "woman," not a "lady." In my politically correct lexicon of that era, "ladies" were helpless, fancy, pampered, and mostly useless. I'm happy to report that I am no longer encumbered by such narrow-minded notions. You were neither helpless nor fancy, much less pampered and useless. You were gentle and genteel, qualities I have come to admire. And yet . . . I still see you as fragile. I still want to protect you. That, I suspect, will never change.

Perhaps a better word than fragility is delicacy. I can't get past your soft manner, your unassertive step, your smooth hands even in age, your aura of delicacy. Yet I know you were strong and uncomplaining. Life threw you some curve balls, but you never let them get the best of you. Take your macular degeneration, for example. I repeat myself, but I am reminded of it again as I contemplate your courage through trials. You refused to feel sorry for yourself, and you continued to function as though nothing was amiss.

Bittersweet

Wanting no one's pity, you took pains to hide the fact that your vision was hopelessly compromised, allowing you to see only blurry images. Your wallet was divided into separate sections for ones, fives, tens, and twenties (I never saw a bill larger than a twenty in your possession). You could tell by its location the monetary value of whatever bill you removed to pay a grocer or a pharmacist. Your coins were similarly separated so that you would not mistake a penny for a dime or a nickel for a quarter. You memorized dozens of phone numbers and learned to recognize even casual acquaintances by their voices. And you took care of Dad through two cancer surgeries, chemotherapy, radiation therapy, and in the end, dementia.

I can still see you reading with a small eyeglass that enabled you to focus, in a limited way, the peripheral vision in your left eye. The device reminded me of a jeweler's glass. It took several months for you to train that eye; but you persisted and finally you read, by moving the text across that eyeglass and putting words together a few letters at a time. (And how did you manage after you fell and broke a bone in your right hand?) You were never one to give up, Mother. I sometimes wonder how your arms supported heavy books, like that large print *Book of Mormon*, through hours and hours of laborious effort. Would I have paid the price to read sacred text? I'd like to think I would, but then, who knows?

Marilyn Arnold

I saw the struggle to function with limited vision get to you only once, though I'm sure you had private moments of frustration and despair. It was in the Orem house. You were in the kitchen, preparing to pour something into a plastic container for refrigerator storage. What your eyes did not tell you was that the lid had not been removed from the container. As you poured the slightly thick liquid, it hit the lid and began running over the cabinet and onto the floor. You broke into tears. I don't think you realized that I had entered the kitchen.

That little incident, indicative as it was of your frustration and challenge, undermined your resolve for that short minute. I should have put my arms around you and held you, but I didn't. Now I ask myself, why on earth didn't I? What was the matter with me? I think I mumbled something and helped clean up the spill, tears in my own eyes that you never saw. I believe you were a bit embarrassed that I had witnessed that brief crumbling, and maybe I was too. Self-pity was an indulgence you seldom, if ever, permitted yourself, Mother. And you certainly had no patience with it in your children. Growing up as you did in a household of eleven people, plus two or three intermittent "boarders" (and no indoor plumbing!), trained you well in the school of the stiff upper lip.

Bittersweet

Macular degeneration was not your only physical challenge, Mother. You were high strung, as they say, and your only daughter has followed your example (or inherited your nature). Even before you retired, before you left Ogden, if I remember right, you began experiencing episodes of atrial fibrillation (as I have done). At the time, since none of us had ever heard of the disorder when it descended on you, it seemed rather exotic and unusual. (These days, we know that heart arrhythmia is not all that uncommon in the older population. Fibrillation, however, can in some cases be quite serious.) You took medication that was supposed to help, and maybe it did at first. I remember times in the Orem house, however, when an episode literally wiped you out for days. We were all relieved when such episodes ended and your heart returned to more normal beating. What we didn't realize at the time was that a return to rhythm could trigger a major stroke.

Which is precisely what happened one fateful day after I had moved to the desert. During a period of slow, off-beat fibrillation, blood can pool and form clots. Then, when the heart suddenly launches into a strong beat, it can send a clot to the brain. You were busy sorting laundry at the kitchen table when a clot broke loose and slammed into your brain. You collapsed on the instant. Dad, who was well into dementia by this time, became aware that something was wrong when you didn't answer his call from his front room chair, but his foggy mind knew nothing of 911. Groping about in a paper-filled drawer, he found a phone number written large and he managed to dial it. (Yes, you still used a rotary dial phone because you were accustomed to it, and it had very large numbers.) The number Dad found happened to belong to your niece's land line, and someone there recognized his voice.

Dad hung up when he couldn't identify the person on the other end, but that person sent my cousin to check on things and she found you unconscious. A quick 911 call brought help, and you did not die, Mother; but your life was changed forever. Virtually destroyed. Your vision worsened, and your body never regained agility and strength. Your life of independence was finished. It didn't seem fair. You who had overcome so much were now overcome.

I rehearse these things because they not only tell your story, but they also explain why I take a daily supplement for my eyes (doctor's orders), eyes which have already started down the path yours took. And why, when atrial fibrillation went from moderate to extreme in my heart, I submitted to ablation, a surgical procedure virtually unknown and highly experimental in your day. Even now, there were no guarantees, the surgeon said; but there was a chance. The process involved threading five wires up the femoral arteries and electrically sealing off misfiring impulses in the left atrium of my heart. If the surgery were successful, the heart would begin beating normally; and within a few months the risk of stroke would diminish measurably.

After four hours attached to an assortment of million-dollar machines, I awakened to new life. That was nearly two years ago. There are still no guarantees, but every month that passes with normal heart action is a plus. Could this have spared you many difficult years, Mother? I can't help wondering, though such wondering is fruitless. Then, too, the surgery might have seemed more daunting to you than your unpredictable heart. You were no coward, but you were cautious, too. Ablation might have sounded too much like hocus-pocus to you.

Well, I seem to have bogged down in the medical pages of this memoir. Having reached full-blown senior citizenship (which was never going to happen to me, the energizer bunny incarnate), I notice that matters of health—mainly the lack thereof—seem at times to dominate the conversations of my peers. Many informal gatherings these days open with a round of medical reports, mine included. Did you notice that, too, Mother? Ah well. Call it a major component of the Maturity Syndrome.

And now, of course, television, at least in the news segments (thank goodness for public radio and television, my mainstays, though never yours), feeds our medical frenzy with seemingly non-stop commercials for prescription and OTC drugs. Count it a blessing that you, who faithfully watched (i.e., listened to while sitting in front of) Eyewitness Evening News, don't have to suffer through these endless health scares and remedies. I swear, Mother, that the possible side effects described in the drug commercials (which can be a list as long as my left leg) sound much worse to me than any condition said pills are purported to alleviate. I note that death is one of the rarer but still possible side effects of some of those miracle drugs. An early and unscheduled journey to heaven (or the other place) would not be the kind of miracle I look for.

We all appear to want a quick fix for our ills these days, regardless of what they are—physical, mental, social, professional, or spiritual. Don't bother us about healthy eating and daily exercise of both body and brain. Such things require too much effort. Just give us a pill or a cure-all supplement, and the internet and iPhone. Now you, Mother, were a walker, as I said—at least two miles a day, even with bad vision and the hazards of unseen obstacles on the sidewalk. A vibrant inspiration you were, until that stroke changed everything in a split second. From there you slid downhill into death. It took four years, that slide, and it was no fun for either of us. But you were still an inspiration. And are to this day an inspiration.

Bittersweet

Marilyn holding cherries at the duplex shared with her parents, while her mother, Rhoda, gives backup support.

Marilyn picking cherries. On opposite page: Rhoda with Marilyn and her two daughters-in-law: JoAnn (Rey's wife) and Margaret (Ned's wife). Below: Photo of the duplex.

Bittersweet

Marilyn Arnold

Marilyn backpacking in rain in the high Sierras near Yosemite.

On the opposite page: Marilyn (on right) backpacking the Paria Canyon in the Utah desert.

Bittersweet

Marilyn Arnold

Skiing with Ned's sons in 1983: Brad, "Aunt Marilyn," Blake, David, and Steve. The three older boys were on the "Mud" trip six years earlier. On the following two pages are notes from Brad and Blake after the Mud trip in 1977. Blake, Ned's oldest son, is now a radiologist and Brad is a pediatrician.

Bittersweet

august 19th 1977

Dear, Aunt Marilyn
Thank you very much for taking us on the outing It was really alot of fun Thanks agian you are the very best aunt. In the world.

Thursday Brad and I went swimming.

And to day I went bowling and got two spares.

Love, Blake

Marilyn Arnold

Dear Aunt Marilyn Thank you for taking me up to The cabin. I had a fun time up there. you are oun of my Best Aunts. I Love you very much.

Love Brad

Page Ten

The day came when it was time for me to move on, to leave the duplex we shared (and the daily acquaintance with cherry trees and other edibles in our big backyard). Your youngest sister, shockingly widowed in her fifties, came to occupy the north side of the duplex for a few years. A good transition period for both of you. I felt like a deserter, and you weren't quite prepared for me to leave. My first move was to Provo, nearer my work at the university. I still picked the cherries, and you and Dad still dried them. It wasn't as though I had moved a great distance. But within a few years I was ready to move again, to a quieter scene with two friends. We built a lovely home on deeply wooded acreage in the mountains. Another adjustment for you and Dad because I was now a good forty-five minutes away. Another guilt trip for me.

But it turned out all right once you got used to it. Our home in Woodland Hills became a happy gathering place where you and Dad loved to come. I can still see Dad

Marilyn Arnold

reclining on the large rear deck, gazing into the maples and oaks with great pleasure and peace. "I just love it here," he used to say. All through the pleasant months from Spring through Fall, you and Dad came out almost weekly for "supper on the deck." You, Mother, brought your special baked beans or potato salad, or both. I grilled hamburgers or pork steaks. We wandered a bit, perhaps gathering a bunch of watercress at the spring, or we simply sat and talked to the accompaniment of crickets and night birds while darkness came on. Occasionally a deer would approach and turn its dark, curious eyes on us before slipping back into the woods. He would postpone his feast in our garden until another day. It was idyllic.

We had captured a magic moment that seemingly could stretch into infinite years. We would all live forever like this. We would not grow older, we would not suffer strokes, or cancer, or dementia but would continue in this enchanted bubble of peace and comradery until the Second Coming, when we would be swept into eternity together, in the twinkling of an eye. It almost seemed so, at least in those hours when we were mesmerized by our good fortune and the coloring sky of sunset overhead.

In those days, it didn't seem to matter that we didn't share our fears verbally, or our doubts, or our secret sadnesses, or our deepest thoughts. What we had together was enough. I wonder why, as the years stacked up behind me, I

Bittersweet

began feeling that we could have had more. Why did I begin wishing I had known you in ways that I never did? Is it that craving, Mother, that produced this book? If so, maybe this book and its full load of newly found memory will finally have satisfied that craving.

The process of remembering is instructive, and I see now that I have no (and never had) grounds for complaint. If you were here, I'd dance you around the kitchen floor, as I should have done years ago. Even then, despite our practiced reserve, we were certainly no strangers, Mother. My work was demanding, and your life full, but we managed to find time for each other, especially in the longer days of summer.

There were the trips to Nebraska, to the childhood home of Willa Cather and the scene of many a national literary conference or seminar in which I was involved. When your last-born son and his family moved to Grand Island, Nebraska, the three of us (you, Dad, and I) drove together to his home (that is, Dad drove, you rode shotgun, and I put the finishing touches on lectures and discussions while sprawled across the back seat of your big brown Ford Ltd). From Grand Island I would travel south to Red Cloud (Cather's hometown) or to Hastings to fulfill my responsibilities among my academic colleagues, most of whom became valued friends over the years. (In the last three years, I have lost two of them, Sue Rosowski and Merrill Skaggs, to early deaths. Sore losses.)

Those trips were lovely, unmarred by a single unkind word or selfish thought. You always packed savory lunches, Mother, and I invariably arrived at our destination stuffed, as a good friend would say, to my "silly gills." What did we talk about, across the long, windy (that's *windy,* as in horizontally moving air, not *windy*, as in curvy roads) miles of Wyoming, and the flat green plains and farmlands of Nebraska? I don't recall a single conversation.

It doesn't matter. We were together, and Dad's mind and body still worked. You seemed happy and contented. I think you were. If I had not had professional responsibilities in Nebraska, I wonder if we would have made those trips together. Perhaps once. Perhaps not at all. I suspect that you would have flown to see your four grandsons (oh yes, and your son and daughter-in-law, who were well-loved, but were not the main attraction), as you did when they lived in Canada and Australia and Pennsylvania. I would have flown to my conferences, or driven with a colleague.

Even now, I find myself smiling to remember those trips to Grand Island. I can't forget the young boys waiting for me, at dusk, with a basketball in their hands. They wouldn't start without me, you remember, and we played on their wide, lighted driveway well into the night. Often neighbor boys joined us, waiting also. (They knew the procedure. We start

Bittersweet

when Aunt Marilyn gets back from her meetings in Red Cloud or Hastings, not before.) I loved to play basketball, and regularly got up games with those same nephews when they entered BYU as students, both before and after their missions. One year all three of them were enrolled at the same time. We also hiked and skied together. As I said, they were the sons I never had, and I still claim them as my own.

I mentioned above your enthusiasm—nay, *passion*—for BYU basketball. As it turned out, for a good number of years (during my administrative stints) I had two sets of tickets for home games. Chances are, if left to myself, I would not have attended all the games, much less have purchased a set of tickets when I already had a couple of freebies (my other perks were good campus parking and a Christmas turkey). But . . . you, Mother. How could I not indulge you? You still attended every game, snow or shine, even after your eyes failed you. A friend who had the seats next to you and Dad gave a running commentary about who was doing what on the floor, and you cheered with the rest of the crowd. (I think Dad became a BYU fan in self-defense and to keep the peace at home.) My complimentary seats were elsewhere, but we drove in together so long as I lived nearby. After that a niece and her husband generously transported you with them.

I didn't say so to your Utah County sisters, who were

probably under the impression that you moved from Ogden to be near them (and possibly me); but privately I suspect that for you, proximity to BYU basketball was reason enough to move to Utah County. At least it sweetened the move considerably. And then, in the years when you and Dad sat in my press box seats at football games (I preferred to sit outside in the weather with a hardy male friend), you were protected from the elements though not from the dignitaries. There you were served lunch, no less, with all the trimmings. You thought you had died and gone to heaven. (Thank goodness, the actual event was still years away, though it came soon enough.)

Yes, come it did, that day I dreaded. The aftermath of that day is still with me. Vivid yet are a few memories of things—not big things, but tangible things—inseparably connected with you. Why do a few things left in your wake at the Orem house stick in my mind while others have disappeared with the years? What a strange matter it was, Mother, to empty drawers you had filled with personal items, and closets hung with clothes you left behind when at last you moved to a care center. Church clothes you would never wear again. Silky blouses with high ruffled collars. Skirts and jackets, shrunk now to fit what age and osteoporosis had done to your once moderate frame. Just looking at the clothes that were so much

Bittersweet

you—I had seen you in every piece—was hard for me. I called in your sisters to rescue me, and they did.

But the drawers. I had to face the drawers alone. Unlike my own desks and chests of drawers, they were orderly and smelled like linens and lilac and faded handkerchiefs. I need to tell my nephews that when I die, they are simply to turn my drawers upside down in a Hefty bag. No examining the worthless junk and exclaiming among themselves that they would not have expected Aunt Marilyn to keep all those dry ballpoint pens, or those crusty rubber bands, or those old keys, or all the rest of the stuff. (No, no, fellas, just dump it all. Don't try to sort it. My one niece would confirm my injunction, though she will probably still be living in far off Alaska and therefore absent and unable to give a feminine defense. But you do have a mother, and you have wives. Ask them. They're on my side.)

The top drawer of the chest beneath the window in your basement bedroom was full of greeting cards. You, Mother, had saved personal greeting cards for years. Birthdays, Mother's Days, other special occasions and thank you's. There among them I saw my own handwriting on long ago envelopes, delivered in person with gifts or mailed from afar. I opened one or two, but couldn't continue. My eyes wouldn't cooperate. Myself, I tend to keep such cards only if I plan to answer them sometime or other. Yes, you guessed it. Most of them go unanswered despite my best intentions. I write and write, all the time, but I don't seem to write many letters and notes. It's a wonder I have any friends left. (My relatives, however, are stuck with me, and they have adjusted over the years—mainly.)

A few of your things I kept, Mother. Too precious they were to give away. Some of those things are in the category of the summer pajamas you made for me, those checked ones I spoke of earlier. It just occurred to me that someone is going to have to dispose of those pajamas when I'm gone. I won't be able to part with them myself. Will that disposer person know why I've kept them when it's been years since I slept in anything fancier than an oversized T-shirt? I'm not sure I want those pajamas relegated to the big Hefty. Maybe a grand niece would want them.

Or maybe they could become part of a quilt. I have slept for years beneath the remnants of home-made clothes I wore in childhood. Grandma Clark, your mother and my snoring partner, stitched the pieces into splendid designs and quilted them. See how sentimental I am at heart? Then there's the embroidered picture of the three owls I described before. I love those owls, and they are currently on display in my laundry room where I smile at them many times daily. (Save the owls, guys. One of the great-granddaughters will treasure them, trust me.)

Bittersweet

Priceless to me is the small (pinky finger) ring that you wore on special, dress-up occasions. It is silver and quietly elegant, like you, my silver-haired mother. As a child I thought it absolutely beautiful, something a queen would wear, or at least a duchess. I like to think that the scarcely visible stone it bears may be a tiny diamond, but your legendary thrift tells me it is merely a rhinestone. (I'm entitled to my little fantasies, Mother.) You gave that ring to me, along with two or three other things, one day near the end of your life. You also gave me a little umbrella your grandmother had given you. Now I must find someone to bestow it upon. Which of your great-granddaughters would think it precious, I wonder?

A blue day it was, with your life winding down and the move to assisted living drawing ominously near. I arrived to find you dolefully sorting through a few of your small treasures to determine which child should have which. You had written names on the little boxes, legible despite your blurred vision, so there would be no mistaking your wishes. No wonder you shed a few tears. How does anyone face what you were facing? On the other hand, how does one avoid it? I have always said, "Better the quick death." (I think I borrowed that phrase from Ray Bradbury.) But then, most of us don't get to arrange our departures, quick or slow, do we?

Marilyn Arnold

And now, more than a decade downstream from your death, I find that I am still vulnerable to sudden rushes of feeling. The other day, as I was looking for some family history materials, I opened a box without thinking. There, Mother, were the clothes you died in. Navy blue polyester pants and white, two-button polo shirt with thin navy blue stripes. Far too small for me, and so full of you during that last inscrutable hour of your life. I wasn't prepared for such a poignant reminder, and I dropped to the floor with your clothes pressed to my face and wept—for love, for loss, for the past, for missed opportunities to comfort you and be comforted. There, too, was the hand-knit shawl you wore to warm your shoulders in the temple. And your favorite dress shoes, a pair of patent leather pumps. Why did I keep those pumps? I asked myself. For the same reason that I have them yet, in their green box with the yellow lid: because I cannot bear to part with them.

How I still cling to you, Mother. Many times a day I pass the official portrait of you and Dad, taken to mark your fiftieth wedding anniversary. Sometimes I pause, pick up the 5 x 7 framed picture, and greet you silently. Your uncertain eyes were not quite focused on the camera, but you are elegant and beautiful. Dad is solemn and solid. The picture is faded, but I can't put it away. I have lived for years in bright, many-windowed houses in the desert, and the sun has taken its toll on that picture (just as it has on me).

Bittersweet

But in that same cabinet where I came onto your blue slacks and striped polo shirt, there is also a box of other pictures. Among them is a photo portrait of you in your early or middle twenties. You look like a movie star of an earlier era, modest black fur drape, dark wavy hair, smooth skin, clear penetrating eyes. I carry that picture in my head. But you, Mother, the unfaded essence of you, I carry in my heart. And will carry every day, every week. Until I greet you some fine morning when I, too, leave shoes (more likely beat-up sandals), a pair of pants (more likely long shorts or jeans), and a shirt (more likely a scruffy T-shirt) for someone to fold up and put in a box—or toss into a Hefty.

Marilyn Arnold

Official photograph of Marilyn Arnold, "the dean" in the deanery.

About the Author

Marilyn Arnold is the author of eight published novels (three for Mayhaven Publishing) and numerous other books, articles, and essays. Known for her wit among readers of all ages, she is also a nationally recognized literary scholar who has lectured widely across Utah and throughout the country. After a distinguished career as a university professor of English, assistant to the university president, and graduate school dean, she has left formal university life and moved to her beloved red rock desert in southern Utah. There she continues to write, lecture, teach, and to serve on various community boards and committees. For many years, she has led book discussions throughout the state for the Utah Humanities Council. When "at rest," she likes to hike, ski, and play tennis.

Marilyn Arnold

Lecturing at the national Willa Cather seminar in Hastings, Nebraska.

Hiking into the Provo cirque.

Marilyn Arnold

Marilyn (on right) and friend on Timpanogos Peak (about 11,750 feet elevation), a rugged climb northeast of Provo, Utah.

Bittersweet

The author hiking somewhere in the Utah desert ("I can't remember where—I've hiked so many gorgeous places.").

Marilyn Arnold

Universe photo by Nadine Spillman

Marilyn Arnold, assistant professor in English, has fun in spite of a broken leg.

Tennis enthusiast not 'aced' by broken leg

By GLENN KIMBALL
Universe Staff Writer

Dr. Marilyn Arnold is proving that tennis is fashionable this year no matter what shape a person is in—literally.

Miss Arnold, assistant professor of English, broke her leg in five places last March doing her thing on the slopes.

A broken leg has been quite a handicap for the sports-minded Dr. Arnold, who said, "I felt blue—especially every time I passed the tennis court."

Three weeks ago she got a brilliant idea as she saw a chair with wheels on it in her doctor's office. So the next thing you know the tennis community was shocked to see a wheel chair racket woman smashing forehands and backhands at Marge Smith, a former Women's tennis team member.

is a bucket full of balls to keep from having to chase them too often, and a sturdy right tennis sneaker because she said, "I have worn out one right tennis shoe already." Include a fast chair and one is in business.

Dr. Arnold, a self-proclaimed outdoor worshiper said, "being able to play tennis has made all the difference in the world this summer."

"Marge and I were formerly ranked second in the state in doubles competition," said Dr. Arnold. "We plan to practice and enter the Women's Open Doubles State Competition in Salt Lake next week... We don't plan to do very well," said Dr. Arnold,

Author, Marilyn Arnold, finding a way to play, even in a cast. Photo and story reprinted with permission, courtesy of Brigham Young University *Daily Universe.*

Bittersweet

The author in her "Desert Rat" Scout.

Fiction by Marilyn Arnold

Desert Song

Fields of Clover

Minding Mama—winner of Mayhaven's Award for Fiction
Mayhaven Publishing, Inc.

Perfecting Amiable
Mayhaven Publishing, Inc.

Sky Full of Ribbons

Song of Hope

The Classmates

Unidentified Lying Objects
Mayhaven Publishing, Inc.

Nonfiction by or with Marilyn Arnold

A Chorus for Peace: A Global Anthology of Poetry by Women

A Reader's Companion to the Fiction of Willa Cather

Bittersweet: A Daughter's Memoir

Book of Mormon Reference Companion

Pure Love: Readings on the Sixteen Enduring Virtues

Sacred Hymns of the Book of Morman

Sweet Is the Word: Reflections on the Book of Mormon

Willa Cather: A Reference Guide

Willa Cather's Short Fiction